SIMPLE
SELF-DEFENSE

Jennifer Lawler

Wish Publishing
Terre Haute, Indiana
www.wishpublishing.com

LCCN:

Editorial assistance provided by Dorothy Chambers
Cover designed by Phil Velikan

Printed in the United States of America
10 9 8 7 6 5 4 3 2 1

Published in the United States by
Wish Publishing
P.O. Box 10337
Terre Haute, Indiana 47801, USA
www.wishpublishing.com

Distributed in the United States by
Cardinal Publishers Group

Some of this material originally appeared in *The Self-Defense Deck*.

Disclaimer

The author, illustrator and publisher accept no responsibility for injuries sustained or inflicted, or damage of any sort that may occur as a result of reading or following the information given here. Reading about and practicing the techniques in no way guarantee that you will be able to use the techniques effectively in any particular self-defense situation. The information in this book deals with handling risky, volatile and violent situations. The author, illustrator and publisher cannot guarantee outcomes or predict human behavior. However, the concepts and principles contained here are sound and reasonable, and based on current self-defense information. As with any physical activity, there is a risk of injury from accidents or overexertion. Get a medical checkup before engaging in physical training programs, including this one.

Introduction

When I finally learned to stand up and defend myself, instead of locking myself indoors after dark and huddling under the covers, I stopped being afraid for the first time in my life. While this increased confidence – not to mention improved self-esteem – was the result of several years of martial arts training, it doesn't have to take years to learn that you can take care of yourself no matter what happens. In *Simple Self-defense*, I'll show you simple but significant strategies you can use to survive a potential attack and feel confident that you can handle any challenges you may face.

Having power in your life comes from knowing what to do next, by analyzing the situation to see what you *can* do next. Being angry or afraid or in a rage doesn't give you power. Being clear in your mind does. Power doesn't come from listening to alarmists who tell you, "Don't go out alone," or "Don't go out at night," or "Don't let anyone know you live alone." Not only do these scare tactics force women to live circumscribed lives, they're also ineffective. Many – perhaps even most – women are hurt by people they know. Very few self-defense books on the market deal with that reality. Those that do give it a passing consideration, then go back to explaining how to dismember the psycho mugger they imagine is your greatest threat. But what if the person hitting me happens to be my husband and the father of my three children? Is blowing him away a reasonable and realistic answer?

A *USA Today* poll showed that 92% of women say that reducing violence and rape is the number-one top-priority issue for them, more important than child care or health care or equal pay for equal work, which we know are hot-button issues, too.

The *USA Today* survey, like others, reveals that the vast majority of women worry about themselves or their loved ones becoming victims of violent crimes, and for good reason: Nearly 14% of women in the U.S. report having been raped at some time during their life. Most assault victims are women or girls under the age of 25. More than half of all forcible rapes occur when the victim is under age 17. And more than two-thirds of sexual assaults go unreported, according to the National Crime Victimization Report.

In only 22% of rapes were the victims assaulted by someone they had never seen before or did not know well. The others were raped by husbands, ex-husbands, boyfriends, ex-boyfriends, fathers, stepfathers, other relatives, friends and neighbors. In cases of rape occurring after the age of 18, 76% of assailants were intimate partners, and 17% were acquaintances, according to the National Women's Study.

Women are also victims of nonsexual violent crimes such as assault and battery. The Gina Eisenman Foundation reports that every eight seconds a woman is battered in the United States. Thousands of American women are murdered by friends, family members, boyfriends or spouses every year. Child abuse, elder abuse and parent-battering also occur among family members and close relatives. Unfortunately, according to the Justice Department's Bureau of Justice Statistics, one in three Americans injured in a violent crime reports that their attacker had committed a crime against them before.

Most books that treat the issue of self-defense consider it a physical response to physical threats. Someone tries to punch you, you punch them back, and whoever has been training harder wins. Yet this approach doesn't always engage women – they're not sure they can do it. It doesn't address the fact that maybe punches don't even need to be thrown. And it teaches women to do things like shove their car keys into their attacker's eyes. Yeah, you're going to do that to your father if he smacks you.

Often, these approaches encourage women to rely on some method or weapon outside themselves – a can of mace, a cell phone – to stay safe. Well, that can of mace is illegal in a lot of jurisdictions, and unless you wear it strapped to your thigh, it's not always going to be available. I don't know of too many attackers who'll let you rummage through your purse while you try to find it. Attacks can happen quickly. Even trained professionals (such as police officers) sometimes get taken by surprise and can't draw their firearms in time. And no matter how careful you are, sometimes your cell phone can't get a signal (or the batteries have died). By focusing on mental preparedness and techniques that almost anyone can do, *Simple Self-Defense* empowers women to feel strong and to know that they can take care of themselves.

The belief that if a woman fights back, she will always lose is also out of touch with reality. In fact, studies show that as many as 50% of attempted crimes of violence can be stopped by the act of shouting!

The fact is, most women are stronger and possess more self-defense skills than they realize – they just don't call them self-defense skills. They range from outsmarting and outwitting an assailant to de-escalating a tense situation to hitting an attacker over the head with your Kate Spade purse (yes, a woman I know has fended off an attacker that way).

This reality-centered approach does not rely on alarmist misinformation or perpetuating paranoia. It offers strategies that require brains and intelligence as well as brawn.

Simple Self-Defense gives women and girls ideas and skills they can use to defend themselves against the big bad world without telling them that they must use a certain technique or they must fight a certain way. It gives women resources for getting out of a bad situation without blaming them for getting into it. Someone else's violence is not your fault. Only the woman defending herself can decide what is right for her to do under the circumstances. But *Simple Self-Defense* will empower you by offering a range of choices, many of them *not* physical techniques, that you can use to take control back from the attacker.

We use self-defense — the art of staying safe in the world (and in our homes) — every day. We ask the cable installer for identification before letting him in, we call a cab instead of walking home late at night, and we make sure our doors lock securely. But no matter how hard we try to avoid danger, life is unpredictable, and no collection of safety tips can keep us safe all the time. That's why everyone needs to be familiar with self-defense strategies that will help them deal with dangerous circumstances. For example, what if cabs don't operate in your town? What do you do then? Or what if it's your boyfriend who's trying to rape you? The lock on the front door can't protect you from that. That's why you need self-defense strategies.

You have probably already developed some strategies to help you feel confident and stay safe in your daily life. Maybe you choose to live in an apartment building with a security guard, or maybe you only park in well-lit areas. *Simple Self-Defense* builds on these practices. It demonstrates different ways to think about self-defense and gives you simple techniques to use if you feel threatened, whether by a stranger or a known attacker. Although the instructions assume a male attacker and a female defender, the techniques in *Simple Self-Defense* can be used by either male or female defenders, and are equally effective in either case.

While this book is intended to offer straightforward strategies and tips for handling self-defense situations, remember that there really are **no** do's and don'ts – you do whatever you have to do, including consciously complying with your attacker. Women have been successfully defending themselves for eons using their own wits and creativity. Using any of these techniques alone won't be as effective as a combination of verbal, psychological and physical techniques, so plan to develop sets of strategies that you can use. Most importantly, being attacked is never your fault. Anyone who survives an attack is a success story.

This book shows how each strategy works, explains why it's effective, and offers helpful tips. The techniques are divided into four basic categories:

- Planning and setting boundaries. This category includes ways to sidestep a potentially dangerous situation before it has a chance to escalate. Learning to set boundaries can protect you from a random mugger as well as a violent boyfriend. If you learn to walk away, you can avoid many threats.

- Nonviolent strategies. This category shows how to use nonphysical, nonviolent strategies to avoid or escape an attack. Projecting a confident image, for example, can reduce the likelihood of an attack. Focusing on what you can do, rather than what you can't, allows you to use your creativity and ingenuity to escape a threatening situation.

- Basic physical techniques (which require little or no preparation). This category describes basic physical techniques that you can use in self-defense situations if you need to reinforce your boundaries with fighting techniques. Knowing the techniques will help you feel more comfortable in your environment and make you more confident as you defend yourself, even if only by saying, "No!" Having the ability to fight often means that you don't have to. The section begins with very basic moves and builds from there.

- Advanced physical techniques (which require some practice). This category features advanced techniques, including joint locks and joint manipulations, more difficult kicks and throws, in case more complicated physical techniques are required to escape from an attacker. These will require practice to perform effectively, especially when you're frightened. Finally, the complicated issue of weapons — defending yourself against them as well as using them — is addressed.

From all of these options, you can choose the most appropriate combination of strategies for your particular situation. You can focus on the particular approaches that make the most sense for you, combining several strategies to increase your safety.

All of the techniques will come more naturally and be more effective if you practice them. Playacting boundary setting with friends, for example, will help you feel comfortable when doing it in a real-life situation. When practicing the physical techniques — the punches, kicks and throws — go slowly at first. Walk through the techniques step by step until you feel confident moving faster. Don't use full power against a practice partner. Instead, use padded targets, such as a heavy bag, pillows or specially designed kicking targets. Take a class with a professional self-defense instructor for hands-on training.

You can practice the techniques on your own, too. For example, you can do the kicks by yourself, "shadow fighting" until you learn how to perform the techniques correctly. Practice balancing on one leg, which is necessary when you kick. You don't have to spend hours on it every day. A few minutes practicing in the morning or before you go to bed at night may be all you need to gain confidence and a working knowledge of basic self-defense strategies that could save your life.

Strategy #1
BE YOUR OWN HERO

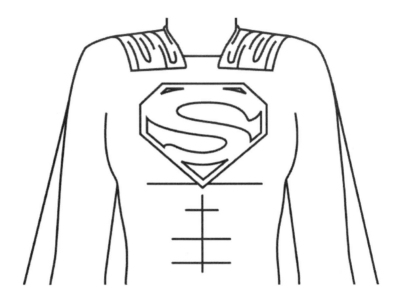

One of the most important concepts in thinking about self-defense is the willingness to take responsibility for your own protection. That does not mean that you shouldn't plan to dial 9-1-1, scream for help, or ask your neighbor to give you a hand if needed. It does mean making plans about what you can do and what you're willing to do (and not do). It's important not to fall into the habit (or trap) of assuming that someone else or something else will take care of it for you. A common error in self-defense thinking is to say, for instance, "Well, we have security alarms on the doors and windows to the house." That's certainly a good start, but you'll also want to think about what happens if that system malfunctions, you forget to set it, and so on. "Be your own hero" does not mean spending all your time focusing on worst-case, doom-and-gloom scenarios, but simply requires you to think about some options: "I could retreat to the bedroom and climb out the window if someone comes through the front door." This can and should be a reassuring exercise, rather than a frightening one.

Being your own hero also means thinking about what kinds of risks you are most vulnerable to. For example, if you're a young woman who's involved in a lot of dating situations, your risk of encountering date rape is obviously much higher than an older woman who has been married for 20 years. Planning suitable precautions makes you less vulnerable to a self-defense situation and more capable of acting if confronted with one. See Assess Risk, #5 for more on this.

TIP: It is especially common for women to think the men in their lives will protect them – that you'll be safe as long as you can send your husband or your boyfriend downstairs to check out that strange sound coming from the kitchen. Keep in mind, though, that he may in fact be unprepared for a self-defense situation. Also, what will you do if he's staying late at work or out of town? Or what if it turns out that he's the one who is threatening you? Depending on yourself makes you less vulnerable to outside factors that you can't always control.

WHY THIS WORKS: Thinking about self-defense before you need to puts you a step ahead of people who haven't thought through how they might react in a given situation. There's no guarantee that you'll react the way you planned – and that's all right – but giving some thought to your options ahead of time makes it more likely that you'll do *something*, rather than be paralyzed with indecision or doubt.

Self-defense philosophy

Ideally, a good self-defense program should reflect these philosophical points:

1. **No one asks for, causes, invites or deserves to be assaulted.** Women and men sometimes exercise poor judgment about safety behavior, but that does not make them responsible for the attack. Attackers are responsible for their attacks and their use of violence to overpower, control and abuse another human being.

2. **Whatever a person's decision in a given self-defense situation, whatever action she/he does or does not take, that person is not at fault.** Someone's decision to survive the best way she can must be respected. Self-defense classes should not be used as a judgment against a victim/survivor.

3. **Good self-defense programs do not "tell" an individual what she "should" or "should not" do.** A program should offer options, techniques, and a way of analyzing situations. A program may point out what USUALLY works best in MOST situations, but each situation is unique, and the final decision rests with the person actually confronted by the situation.

4. **Empowerment is the goal of a good self-defense program.** The individual's right to make decisions about her participation must be respected. Pressure should not be brought to bear in any way to get someone to participate in an activity if she's hesitant or unwilling.

*Prepared for the National Coalition Against Sexual Assault by the NCASA Self-Defense Ad-Hoc Committee. For more information contact: **NCASA**, National Coalition Against Sexual Assault, P.O. Box 21378, Washington, D.C. 20009*

Strategy #2

TEST YOUR AWARENESS

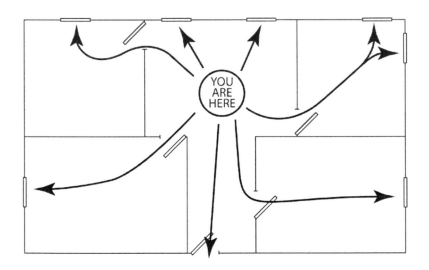

Often people report that they were able to accurately predict a threat by noticing a change in their environment – a car parked in a place on the street where no one usually parks, a "delivery driver" whose uniform didn't quite fit the part. Learning to be aware of your surroundings helps you see a potential threat before it becomes a real problem. Get in the habits of noticing what's typical in your familiar surroundings, and of checking out new environments you go into. What are the people doing? Who is usually home at what times of day? What is the atmosphere like? High levels of tension may mean that conflict is escalating, and noticing that can help you keep your cool and either diffuse the tension or leave the situation.

To test your awareness, you can do simple exercises. These can be fun to do with a friend, challenging each other to be more accurate. Or pretend you're a spy, gathering information to report back to your boss. There's no reason that thinking about self-defense has to be dramatic and scary.

One exercise is the "before" and "after" exercise. Before you leave for work, take a minute to look up and down your street. Then make mental notes about what you remember seeing – who is outside (what are they doing?), where the cars are parked, who has open windows or garage doors. Later, when you return home, do the same thing, only this time identifying any differences that you see.

You can also play a version of the memory game, where you spend 30 or 60 seconds looking at a certain environment, and then close your eyes (or leave the environment) and have someone quiz you about what's happening there. Sample questions might be: Who is outside watering the lawn? At which house is the gray Volvo parked in the driveway?

Building awareness is not about becoming paranoid but about being present in and conscious of your surroundings.

TIP: Don't forget to get in the habit of noticing ways to escape and reach help. For example, when you go into a mall, you can make a note of the various exit locations, the store hours (so you're not wandering around after almost everyone else has gone home), the security guard and pay phone locations (in case you can't get to your cell phone or don't have one) and that type of thing.

WHY THIS WORKS: Building awareness helps you notice changes in your environment and also helps you spot and recognize potential threats for what they are. If you notice that someone's been following you for the last three blocks, you're in a much better position to take action than if you don't notice him until he grabs your arm.

Resources for more information:

Rape, Abuse & Incest National Network (RAINN)
24-hour hotline: 1.800.656.HOPE
www.rainn.org

National Sexual Violence Resource Center
Information, links
www.nsvrc.org

The Ophelia Project
Information, resources for girls
www.opheliaproject.org

Your local rape crisis center, listed in your local yellow
pages phone book under "crisis center," "crisis inter-
vention service" or a similar heading

Strategy #3

BUILD YOUR INTUITION

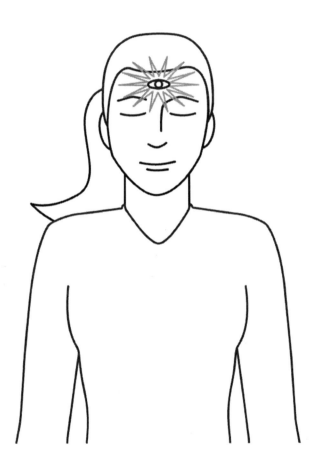

Our intuitions – "gut" feelings about what is happening or could happen – are based on past experience and on biological senses that we're not always aware of (such as the innate sense we have that someone is staring at us). These feelings can be invaluable in keeping us safe from harm because they alert us to potential threats.

The most important thing you can do to build your awareness is to listen to it. Next time you get butterflies in your stomach, stop and give yourself a minute to assess the situation. Are you nervous because you're about to give a major speech, and if it doesn't go well you're going to get fired? Or are you nervous because that guy on the street corner is wearing an overcoat and sweating bullets when it's 90 degrees outside, and you've gotta wonder what's up with him?

The next most important thing you can do to build your intuition is to act on it, which is a way of showing respect for it and learning from it. When you act, you get more information that helps you refine your intuition. For example, suppose you're waiting for the elevator, and a couple of creepy-looking guys get on. Your intuition tells you to wait for the next car (while the "thinking" part of your brain is probably telling you something like, "Now, it's not nice to judge a book by its cover.") Go ahead and act on your intuition. Then assess the situation afterward: "I felt better waiting for the next car, even if nothing would have happened." Or, "Screaming for the security guard to call 9-1-1 may have been an overreaction. Next time it would be better to just walk over to the security stand and wait for the next car there."

REMEMBER: Think about what you did right and acknowledge your instincts and smarts when you get out of uncomfortable or downright hostile situations. "I'm glad I didn't let that guy pressure me into having a drink with him. I didn't feel like it, and even if he didn't intend anything bad, it was a good chance for me to learn how to set and enforce boundaries."

TIP: We can't always measure when we've prevented a self-defense situation. Were those guys in the elevator *really* dangerous? Who knows? So while it's important to think about how you acted on your intuition in a certain situation, *never* feel embarrassed when you take actions to protect yourself.

WHY THIS WORKS: Our brains process a lot of information every day, all day long, comparing this situation to that one, assessing information we get from all of our senses, and only a very small percentage of that information makes it to the level of conscious awareness. Therefore, when you get a "gut instinct" or an intuition, it's probably your brain "noticing" something unfamiliar, dangerous or potentially risky about a situation on a subconscious thinking level. Heeding that warning – or at least listening to it – strengthens your intuition.

AS AN EXAMPLE: While I'm sitting here typing this, my brain notices and dismisses the sounds of traffic outside the window because it's not any kind of threat to me in my current situation. I don't even consciously hear it, although it's there. However, later when I go for a walk to the post office, my brain is going to bring information about traffic noise to my conscious awareness, because it doesn't want me to get run over while I'm crossing the street.

Recommended reading:

- Bart, Pauline B., and Patricia H. O'Brien. *Stopping Rape – Successful Survival Strategies* (Pergamon Press, 1985).

- Caignon, Denise and Gail Groves. *Her Wits About Her – Self-Defense Success Stories by Women* (Harper & Row, 1987).

- Dass, Ram and Paul Gorman. *How Can I Help?– Stories and Reflections on Service* (Alfred A. Knopf, 1999).

- DeBecker, Gavin. *The Gift of Fear* (Dell, 1997).

- Langelan, Martha J. *Back Off – How to Confront and Stop Sexual Harassment and Harassers* (Fireside, 1993).

- McCaughey, Martha. *Real Knockouts – The Physical Feminism of Women's Self-Defense* (New York University Press, 1997).

- Medea, Andra and Kathleen Thompson. *Against Rape* (Farrer, Straus and Giroux, 1972).

- Snortland, Ellen. *Beauty Bites Beast – Awakening the Warrior Within Women and Girls* (Trilogy, 1998).

Strategy #4

SELF-DEFENSE IS LOCAL

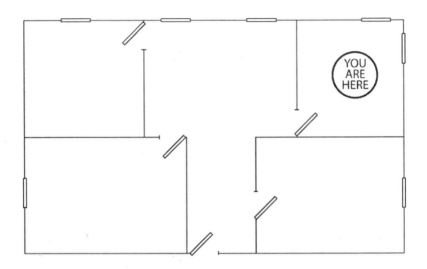

YOU
ARE
HERE

One of the uncomfortable things about traveling is that you're not familiar with the turf, so you don't have a good sense of what's normal and typical in your surroundings and what's not. That's why we tend to be at a higher level of alertness in unfamiliar areas. We perceive them to be riskier to us – and in a sense they are, because we don't know what we don't know.

A person who lives in a small town with very little stranger crime has a different set of self-defense worries from someone living in a big city with a larger amount of stranger crime. Know what your risks are in your local area (see Assess Risk, #5, for more information). For instance, there may be certain parts of town where it would be wise to meet a client during daylight hours in a public area instead of in a private place after dark. The more you know about an area, the easier it is for you to avoid potential threats.

Crime and violence can come in waves and cycles. In some communities, home invasions are becoming increasingly common. If you live in one of those areas, it makes sense to develop plans and strategies for that potential situation. In other areas, such acts are practically unheard of, and you would be better off spending your time developing plans and strategies for more common risks.

TIP: When traveling, do ask locals for their opinions on the safety of various plans and the effectiveness of various strategies you might use. "Is it safe to walk to the drugstore from this hotel? What is the best way to get help if I need it?" Obviously, not everyone's opinion is going to be equally informed and helpful, but getting into the practice of seeking information can help you avoid potentially risky situations.

WHY THIS WORKS: Responding to your environment based on your understanding of what is typical and what isn't can help you stay safe. See Test Your Awareness, #2, for more information.

Strategy #5
ASSESS RISK

When we think about all the potential sources of harm to us, we can get overwhelmed. We may feel that there's really nothing we can do about any of it and thus don't do anything, or we can spend so much time and energy trying to prevent risk that we end up paranoid, not really getting to live our lives or enjoy them to the fullest.

That's why it's important to understand what your risks really are. Intimate partner violence is common; therefore, spending time learning what a healthy relationship looks like and how you can develop one, and identifying potentially harmful ones before you get too involved are some of the smartest self-defense strategies you'll ever use.

By the same token, a woman who lives with a man (whether spouse, boyfriend or relative) is at a higher risk of violence than a woman who doesn't. A younger woman is at a higher risk of violence than an older woman. Women actively dating are at a higher risk of violence than women who are not. Situations that include drugs and alcohol are at a higher risk of escalating into violence than those that do not.

Risks for men are somewhat different: Men are more likely to be the victims of stranger attacks, they are less likely to be the victims of intimate partner violence, and they are more likely to die of violence. Given these circumstances, their self-defense strategies may be a little different.

TIP: Practice likely scenarios, either with friends or simply using your imagination. Consider what you would do in different circumstances, such as a carjacking or a boyfriend slapping you. Make a plan for responding to these different situations.

WHY THIS WORKS: Understanding these risks can help you plan for strategies to avoid potential danger. For instance, considering that dating and alcohol consumption are two areas with a higher risk of violence, combining them may not be a great idea (at least not until you have been dating a specific person for a period of time and have the information and experience needed to trust him).

Strategy #6
CREATE A FAMILY PLAN

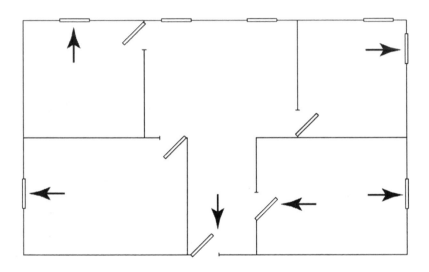

Although the focus of this book is on defending yourself from potential violence, it's important to consider how to deal with potential threats as a family. It's common, for example, for women to be responsible for young children. What would you do if you saw a potential threat while you had your three kids in tow in the parking lot at the mall? The answer may be different from what you would do if you were alone.

Spend some time thinking about ways to reduce the risk of violence to your family as well as to yourself. For example, in the above scenario, one solution would be to simply go back inside the mall and ask for a security guard to escort you to your car.

Creating a family plan can help everyone in your family get on the same page. Just as you plan what to do in case of a fire – including where to meet outside so that you can know everyone is out of the house – you can plan for different self-defense scenarios. Don't make the discussion too frightening, and do ask your children for their input so that you can gently correct any misunderstandings or inappropriate strategies. Do give them concrete ideas: "Always come to Mom's room first if you think you hear someone in the house at night." "If someone is trying to hurt Mommy, call 9-1-1 instead of trying to stop him." Every family's plan will be different depending on your children's ages and what you feel is an appropriate response to a particular self-defense situation.

TIP: While child safety is beyond the scope of this book, do spend some time talking with your children about what they can do personally to stay safe as well. Go beyond the "stranger danger" talk and discuss potential scenarios and what your child could do in various self-defense situations. Even young children can learn to call 9-1-1 and memorize their names, their parents' names, their address and their phone number – information that can be invaluable to anyone trying to help the child. The key is helping them understand when it's appropriate to give this information and to whom it's appropriate to give it.

WHY THIS WORKS: Having a family plan can put your mind at ease. Children often find that actually talking about plans is less frightening than vague worries about what they should do if something "bad" happens. Remember, it takes more than one conversation to develop a family plan, and the plan will change over time as children get older and different risks present themselves.

More recommended reading:

- Belenky, Mary Field, Blythe McVickerClinchy, Nancy Rule Goldberger and Jill Mattuck Tarule. *Women's Ways of Knowing – The Development of Self, Voice and Mind* (Basic Books, 1997).

- DeBecker, Gavin. *Protecting the Gift* (Random House, 1999).

- Evans, Patricia. *Verbal Abuse Survivors Speak Out on Relationship and Recovery* (Adams Media Corporation, 1993).

- Grauerholz, Elizabeth and Mary A. Koralewski. *Sexual Coercion – A Sourcebook on Its Nature, Causes and Prevention* (Lexington Books, 1991).

- Henley, Nancy. *Body Politics – Power Sex and Non-Verbal Communication* (New York, 1977).

- Lawler, Jennifer and Laura Kamienski. *Training Women in the Marital Arts* (Wish, 2007).

- Warshaw, Robin. *I Never Called It Rape* (Harper, 1994).

Strategy #7

FORGET THAT YOUR BRA IS SHOWING

We tend to be self-conscious about doing things that attract attention to ourselves, even if doing such a thing could help keep us safe. We also tend to put ourselves at risk in order to prevent embarrassment. For example, suppose you're getting out of the shower when you realize that someone is climbing in through your bedroom window. You know that running out of your apartment is the safest thing to do, but I guarantee the first thing you will think is, "I can't do that! I don't have any clothes on!"

Many times, being willing to be embarrassed ("What if I'm wrong and I never was in any danger? I'll look like an idiot.") can be the difference between staying safe and not. You may be embarrassed to get off the train when the five kids in gang gear get on, but don't worry about what other people will think. Do what you need to do to stay safe.

TIP: You can also practice being embarrassed, such as by getting off the elevator when the unthreatening elderly lady gets on, just to show yourself that only you are responsible for your actions and that you can choose to do whatever you want or need to do.

WHY THIS WORKS: One of the biggest challenges in responding to a self-defense situation is overcoming the tendency to freeze and not do anything. Fear of embarrassment is one of those things that makes you freeze. If you can practice and plan for doing things that may be embarrassing but may also keep you safe, you're more likely to be ready and able to act when the time comes.

Strategy #8

GOSSIP WITH YOUR GIRLFRIENDS

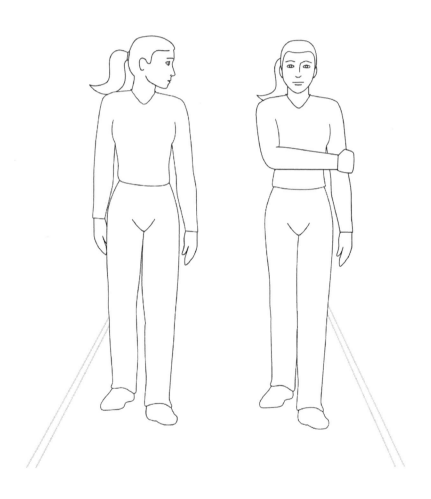

Your BFF is not just a mental health necessity, but she may also be a terrific self-defense partner. You can practice various self-defense strategies with your friends so that you can get an understanding of how they work.

But that's not the only way your friends can help you develop self-defense strategies. You can also just talk to them about what they would do in different risk scenarios. Their ideas may give you ideas that you hadn't thought about before. And sharing experiences, especially about successfully dealing with challenging situations, can bolster your confidence. Many of us have stories of standing up to trouble, or walking away from trouble, or dealing with trouble that we don't necessarily think of as self-defense situations, but the lessons we've learned from them can help us in such situations – and can help our friends, too.

You don't have to plan a "self-defense strategy session." You can just bring it up in everyday conversation. "I had a weird thing happen to me yesterday. I was getting on the bus when . . . . What would you have done?" That can get the ball rolling.

TIP: Be prepared to hear about a friend's encounter with violence or risk that didn't turn out well. Many, many women have stories of rape or abuse, and you wouldn't know it just by looking at them. Listen respectfully and most importantly, do not blame the victim. Understand that surviving an attack is an enormous success, and don't get into a game of second-guessing what she should have done differently.

WHY THIS WORKS: Collectively, we're a lot smarter and have a lot more experience than we do individually. Talking about (and honoring and respecting) all of our various experiences not only helps us feel connected but can help us deal with our own potential risk situations.

Strategy #9

LOOK 'EM IN THE EYE

One of the basic ways we avoid conflict is by not challenging others, and one of the ways we avoid challenging others is by not looking them in the eye. Humans can perceive others looking at/staring at them as a threat. Thus we develop our tendency to avoid eye contact, particularly with strangers, and particularly if we're women.

However, very often you can defuse a potential self-defense situation by looking the other person in the eye – *seeing* him, so to speak. This doesn't mean staring, but it does mean making eye contact. In fact, acknowledging another person can be a simple act of respect that reinforces community and connectedness, which may reduce your risk.

In a confrontation itself, it is also important to maintain eye contact, because watching another person's eyes can give you a sense of what he is going to do next. For example, he's going to look at your arm before he grabs it, giving you the opportunity to step out of the way or at least prepare for the grab.

TIP: Making eye contact with another person can also communicate your self-confidence, which makes you a less attractive victim.

WHY THIS WORKS: You'd be surprised at how often conflict and violence can stem from a person feeling as if he is "invisible" (that is, powerless), or from a person trying to be invisible (that sleazy opportunist doesn't want you watching while he tries to spike your drink with rophynol, the sedative that's used as a date rape drug). Thus, looking him in the eye can help defuse a potentially risky situation.

Strategy #10

GO ALONG TO GET ALONG

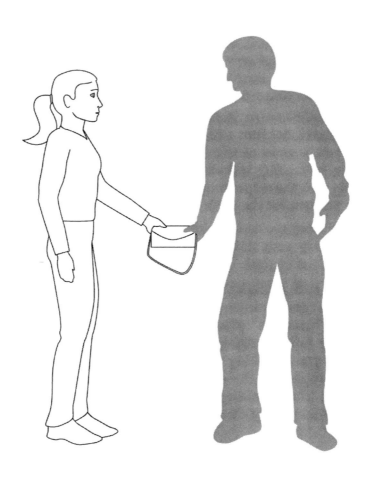

Throughout this book, the strategies I discuss are about actions you can take to help avoid a potentially dangerous situation or to get out of one that you've gotten into. However, it's equally important to remember that sometimes compliance – doing exactly what the attacker wants you to do – is a reasonable course of action.

No one can tell you when you should comply and when (or if) you should fight. That depends on you and the particular situation in which you find yourself. While it can be helpful to plan ahead – for example, you may decide that if someone ever tries to force you into a car, you'll fight as hard as you can – you can't always know how you'll respond if an attack actually occurs. That's okay. Remember that compliance can be an acceptable strategy to use.

TIP: If you do comply in a threatening situation and later second-guess yourself, remind yourself that you did the best you could under the circumstances, and that acting any other way may have been worse.

WHY THIS WORKS: Trying to confront an attacker can sometimes escalate the violence of a situation. For example, if a mugger wants your purse and you resist, he may physically hurt you to get what he wants, whereas if you just let him have your purse, you may have to cancel your credit cards and get your driver's license reissued, but you won't have to deal with any broken bones. Even in more serious assault situations, complying may prevent even worse injury. It is always up to you to do what you think is right in any given situation, and no victim is ever to blame for what happens.

Strategy #11

CONTROL YOUR **BAD SELF**

We've all had the experience of getting into an argument where we end up yelling at the other person, and we can't quite figure out how we got to that point. We may not have noticed the signs that the other person was getting upset about what we were saying, or we were so focused on proving that we were "right" that we didn't care how loud our voices got to make our point.

Confrontations and violence can easily escalate when we don't pay attention to what we're doing and how we're doing it. Since raised voices don't feel good – and can lead to raised fists – it's always a good idea to control your own anger and frustration in any situation before letting it get out of hand.

It's important to recognize when your temper is flaring and your feelings are getting out of control. Instead of giving into them and potentially escalating an uncomfortable situation to a violent one, practice disengaging and letting the situation cool down.

- Try phrases like, "This is getting both of us upset. Let's try again when we've cooled down" or "I don't agree with you, but this isn't getting us anywhere. Let's agree to disagree on this one."

- Don't forget old standbys like counting to 10 or taking deep breaths to help prevent you from saying or doing something you'll regret.

- Walk away (See #23). Sometimes the best way to de-escalate tension is to walk away and cool off.

TIP: You can also learn to recognize signals of anger and frustration in other people. This does not mean you need to appease everyone all the time the instant they show the slightest discomfort, but it can help to say, "Look, I see you're getting upset with what I'm saying, which is not my intention. Let's try again another time, and I'll try to figure out a better way to say it."

WHY THIS WORKS: Sometimes we contribute to potentially dangerous situations by escalating the tension in heated arguments. By de-escalating – recognizing the possibility of the conflict going beyond acceptable boundaries – we can give ourselves a chance to cool down and tackle the problem in another way.

Life strategy tip:

Choose Your Friends Wisely

Most attackers are known to their victims. Therefore, it makes sense to choose your friends wisely. Many people defeat the purpose of expensive burglar alarm systems by befriending the wrong people. Obviously you can't always know whom to trust, but there are often warning signs that we fail to heed. People who are unkind to animals, who admit to being unable to control their violent tempers, or who drink or do drug s should be handled with extreme caution.

Also be careful of friends of friends or acquaintances you don't really know. Sometimes we forget that we don't know a person very well. Get to know these people better before allowing them access to your personal life. Just because you met someone at your sister's party doesn't mean he is a friend.

Strategy #12
KNOW WHAT TO DO NEXT

PLAN B

You wouldn't expect a boxer to go into the ring planning to drop his opponent with one punch. But people very often deal with self-defense situations with this kind of thinking. "I'll just walk away," they may say. Or, "I'll just kick him in the groin." There's nothing wrong with using strategies like that, but you need to have a variety of strategies available in case one particular approach doesn't work in your particular situation.

For example, suppose you're in a disagreement with someone. You're both getting angry, so you wisely decide to de-escalate by controlling yourself (see Control Your Bad Self, #11), but that doesn't stop him; he's still shouting at you, and you think the situation could get even worse. So, again acting wisely, you decide to walk away: "You know, Bob, you're really upset about this. I'm going to head home, and we can talk about this again tomorrow when we're both a little clearer about what we want." But then he grabs your arm. Now what?

You could do a physical defense, such as pulling your arm free or shoving his away (see Push Hands Technique, #20), or you could say, "Let me go right now" (See Saying What You Want, #17). But you need to think about this ahead of time. Always consider what you will do next if your first strategy isn't sufficient or doesn't work.

TIP: Play the "what if" game so that you can consider different ways a self-defense situation could play out. Again, don't make yourself paranoid or scare yourself to death over worst-case scenarios, but look at it in the context of making a plan that will help you get out of trouble should you need to.

WHY THIS WORKS: Planning ahead to use a variety of self-defense strategies means you're less likely to freeze if your first attempt doesn't work as you planned. Having a backup makes you more confident and helps you deal flexibly with a situation that cannot be predicted ahead of time.

Strategy #13

SHOUT IT OUT

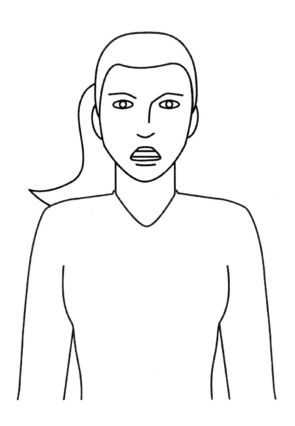

One of the most effective self-defense strategies is being able to shout. It doesn't matter all that much what you shout: "Get away from me!" or "No!" or whatever springs to mind. What matters is that an attacker does not want to have attention drawn to what he is doing, and if you do draw attention to it, very often he'll find someone else to hassle.

Unfortunately, just as much as an attacker doesn't want attention drawn to him, most people don't like to draw attention to themselves either. In martial arts training, the kiai (shout) is something a lot of women have trouble doing at first, because it draws attention to them. But learning how to do it in a martial arts class means you're more likely to be able to shout for help or to yell, "Stay away from me!" in a potential self-defense situation.

TIP: This is one that you really have to practice to get right. A simple way to start is to turn on some music and start singing along, then, once you're going, practice shouting as loudly as you can. The first few times you will probably feel foolish, but after a while it won't bother you at all. You can also practice with friends, but this can be less effective if everyone feels embarrassed and laughs over what they're doing. Having a serious leader (such as at a self-defense class) will make a difference.

WHY THIS WORKS: The more you can draw attention to a potential threat, the more the attacker will want to get away before someone does something that puts *him* in jeopardy. Therefore, doing anything you can to make a commotion can help you.

Strategy #14
COMMITTING YOURSELF

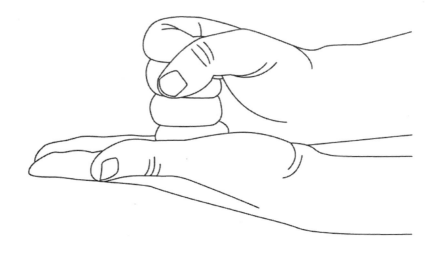

In any self-defense situation, you need to be committed to protecting yourself. This means that if you're going to shout (as in Shout It Out, #13), you need to shout as loudly as you can as many times as you need to. If you're going to physically fight an attacker, then you should be prepared to hit as hard as you can and as often as you need to (and be prepared to get hit, too). In other words, if you really don't think you can hit an attacker with great force, you probably should find another strategy instead.

TIP: Practicing any and all of the strategies ahead of time can help you build the confidence you need to commit to them.

WHY THIS WORKS: Believing in yourself and in your course of action means that you put all of your mental and emotional energy behind what you're doing, which makes you very powerful. Being doubtful and unsure makes you less effective. So be committed to whatever strategy you intend to use in a self-defense situation.

SIMPLE *SELF-DEFENSE*

Strategy #15
ACT IMMEDIATELY

As soon as you see the fist coming, act. Block or counter-attack or run away – it doesn't matter as long as you do something. The key to effective self-defense is to act as soon as you sense a threat. The problem is that people often hesitate, unsure of themselves. That's when the attacker takes control. Delaying an action while you decide whether the attacker has a felony in mind or only a misdemeanor seriously increases the risk to you. While you may sometimes be unsure of whether a threat is truly happening, taking action prevents you from suffering the consequences.

If you know the attacker, that can contribute to your lack of immediate, decisive action. You think, "Good old Joey can't possibly be intending to punch me, can he?" This moment of disbelief can land you into trouble. Rest assured that Joey can be intending to punch you, but that you don't have to stand for it. To overreact – in the sense of getting away, not in the sense of shooting Joey the next time he flinches – is perfectly fine. To underreact is bad for your health.

Instead, go ahead and follow your instincts. If your instincts say, "Duck and run!" then do it, even if it feels foolish. It's good to be whole and sound and feeling foolish. In other words, assume that it is an attack and act accordingly.

TIP: The action you take can be as simple as crossing to the other side of the street or walking back into the store you just left or not getting on the elevator. It could be changing your phone number or calling 9-1-1 or buying a big old dog to bark at people who walk by. It doesn't have to be a complicated jujitsu throw, although it can be.

WHY THIS WORKS: Attackers who are strangers to you count on the element of surprise to move you quickly from where you are to surroundings where they have control. They try to shove you into a car, for example, betting that you'll freeze and not say a word or do anything (like kick 'em). Make that a bad bet for the bad guys by acting the moment you sense trouble. Even a good shriek in the attacker's eardrum can work. If you disrupt this attacker's plans, he'll go hunting elsewhere.

Attackers you're acquainted with often signal their intentions more subtly. They may verbally abuse you or belittle you or make jokes about how they'd stab you through the heart if you cheated on them. (Okay, that one's not so subtle.) If your instincts pick up on these threats, respect your instincts. Take action. Throw the bum out. See a counselor. Do what needs to be done before any violence erupts.

Questions to ask when evaluating a self-defense course, part 1 of 3:

1. **What is self-defense?** Self-defense is a set of awareness, assertiveness and verbal confrontation skills with safety strategies and physical techniques that enable someone to successfully escape, resist and survive violent attacks. A good self-defense course provides psychological awareness and verbal skills, not just physical training.

2. **Does self-defense work?** Yes. Self-defense training can increase your options and help you prepare responses to slow down, de-escalate or interrupt an attack. Like any tool, the more you know, the more informed you are to make a decision and to use it.

3. **Is self-defense a guarantee?** No. There are no guarantees when it comes to self-protection. However, self-defense training can increase your choices/options and your preparedness.

---

4. Is there a standard self-defense course? No. There are many formats for training. They may be as short as two hours or as long as eight weeks or a semester. Whatever the length of the program, it should be based on maximizing options, simple techniques and respect for individuals' experiences.

5. Is there a course I should stay away from? Only you can answer this question. Find out about the philosophy of the program and the background of the instructor. Observe a class session if you can and talk to an instructor or a student. Is the instructor knowledgeable and respectful of your concerns? Is it a length that you can commit to and a cost that you can afford? You deserve to have all your questions answered before taking a class.

6. Who's better, a male or female instructor? For women, there is an advantage to having a female instructor, who has similar experiences surviving as a woman, as a role model. All-woman classes tend to provide an easier atmosphere in which to discuss sensitive issues. On the other hand, some women feel having male partners to practice with can add to their experience. The quality of a class depends on the knowledge, attitude and philosophy of the instructor, not necessarily the gender. The most important aspect is that the instructor, male or female, conducts the training for the students geared to their individual strengths and abilities. Feeling safe and building trust come before learning.

Prepared for the National Coalition Against Sexual Assault by the NCASA Self-Defense Ad-Hoc Committee. NCASA encourages the dissemination of this material with attribution to: National Coalition Against Sexual Assault, P.O. Box 21378, Washington, D.C. 20009

Strategy #16
REFUSING TO ENGAGE

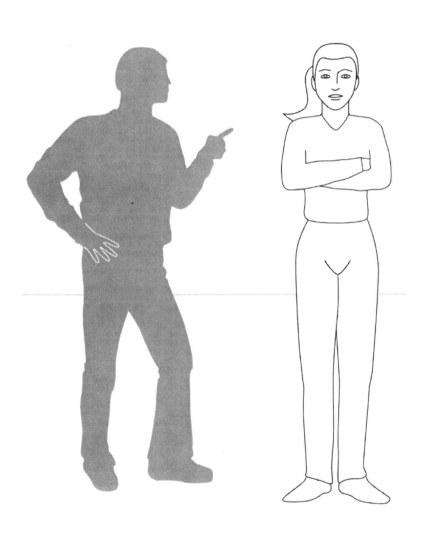

Rapists, stalkers, and other assailants often engage their victims with nonthreatening behavior before attacking. They throw out a verbal "rope" and hope you grab it. They may attempt to get personal information from you. Refuse to reveal personal information to strangers, and put the brakes on conversations that make you uncomfortable, defensive or upset.

- Refusing to engage in conversation with strangers can help keep you safe. You aren't required to respond to anyone's overtures.

- Ignore the conversation. Walk away or pick up a book or magazine to signal that you're otherwise occupied.

- If a conversation with someone you know is getting too heated, simply disengage and say you'll continue the discussion at another time.

- Don't allow others to push your buttons. Don't respond, even if they say provocative things like, "You don't care about the homeless," or "Are you racist?"

TIP: Practice refusing to engage with a friend. Have her push your buttons by making provocative statements ("Why are you such a bitch?") and make it your goal not to answer.

WHY THIS WORKS: Since many attackers rely on their victim's cooperation, by not cooperating, you make it very hard for them to victimize you. They'll try another target if you refuse to engage.

Strategy #17
SAYING WHAT YOU WANT

Establishing clear boundaries shows the offender that he has crossed a line and that you expect him to stop. It also means that no one can use the excuse "I thought you didn't mind." Department of Justice statistics show that many assaults have been stopped by simply shouting, "No!" Attackers don't want to draw attention to themselves. A loud, confident "No!" stops them in their tracks. (See Shout it Out, #13). But there's more to saying what you want than just shouting at a would-be attacker. You need to be very clear in setting your boundaries.

- Tell the person harassing you at work: "I want you to leave me alone," or "Stop that."

- To defuse tension, say, "I don't want to fight."

- Shout, "No!" if someone threatens you in any way, such as by approaching you in a way you find frightening, touching you, grabbing you or hitting you.

- Name the behavior. "This is rape. I want you to stop."

TIP: Use the "broken record" technique. Think of a statement that establishes your boundaries (for example, "I want you to leave me alone," or "Don't come any closer") and then repeat it over and over to the person harassing you.

WHY THIS WORKS: Setting boundaries, particularly with people you know, signals to them (as well as to yourself) that their behavior is unacceptable and must stop. Unfortunately, many people in the world give mixed signals or say one thing and mean another, which is why we have to be clear and repetitive about setting our boundaries so that the offender can eventually hear us and back off.

Strategy #18

IDENTIFYING ABUSERS AND MANIPULATORS

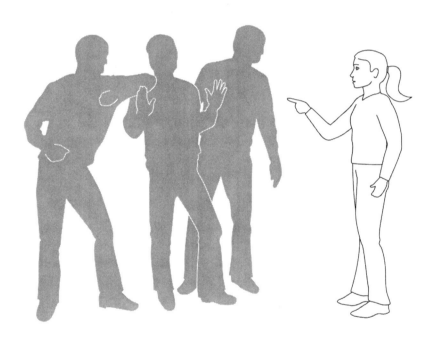

Abusers and manipulators commonly victimize through a series of calculated steps that include intrusion, escalation of coercive behavior (called desensitization) and isolation. They use these techniques because they work – and often the victim never realizes that she was manipulated into that position. If you're aware of the process, you're less likely to fall victim to abusers and manipulators.

The red flags for abusers include:

- Ignoring your feelings

- Not listening to what you say

- Not stopping when asked to stop

- Talking about or looking at your body in a way that makes you uncomfortable

- Touching you inappropriately and without permission

- Blocking your path or following you

- Trying to get you drunk or giving drugs

- Seeming to enjoy your discomfort

- Making comments or jokes about women that are disrespectful

Rape experts state that often no physical force is used in a rape because the process of intrusion/desensitization/isolation works so well. Don't let it happen to you!

TIP: Very often what our society perceives as "romantic" is actually abusive, controlling behavior. Be clear in understanding what a healthy relationship is, and how loving, caring people really act toward each other (and the above list ain't it).

WHY THIS WORKS: Knowledge is power. Being aware that someone is manipulating you makes it nearly impossible for that person to succeed.

Strategy #19
STOP SMILING

When a stranger approaches you at the grocery store to ask you where the cheese is, what's the first thing you probably do? You probably smile, 'cause you're a nice person. And that's fine. But a smile communicates exactly the wrong thing when you're in the middle of a stressful encounter. Instead, work to keep your face and emotions calm and neutral during any conflict. Suppose, for example, the person in the car in front of you slams on his brakes, and you don't have sufficient time to react, so you bump his rear bumper. He leaps out of the car and starts yelling at you. Instead of smiling, trying to placate him and saying, "I'm sorry, I'm sorry," imagine yourself getting out of your car, face perfectly neutral, ignoring his blathering and saying, "Shall we see if any damage has been done?" And then, "Let's call the police to file a report." And that's it. Can you imagine who has the power in that scenario? You do, of course. You're not out of control, you're not sending mixed signals, and you're not agreeing that you're bad, stupid and incompetent.

Equally important, don't let a stranger's smile lull you into thinking he's friendly. More than one evil and demented man has acted like a friendly person shortly before dismembering his victim. Assuming you want to avoid this fate, you should be wary of the true intentions of smiling men.

Smiling is such an ingrained habit for most women that we actually have to practice not smiling. Do this with a friend sometime – actually take some time to role play a stressful encounter in which you keep your face neutral. At first it's hard not to break into laughter, but it's really excellent training.

TIP: During any conflict, think "guard dog." A guard dog doesn't wag his tail. He doesn't necessarily launch himself at the other person's throat, but he waits alertly to see what happens next. He doesn't lick the burglar's face. He growls at the first sign of trouble. So should you.

WHY THIS WORKS: Women often smile as a way to pacify others, or as a nervous reaction to stress. (I have

more than one friend who laughs during funerals because of the stress.) The smile sends the wrong signal to
a potential attacker, identifying you as someone who
could be manipulated and forced to submit since you
seem so eager to please. Keeping your face neutral makes
a potential attacker see that you're not easily intimidated
(it's OK to be shaking inside).

Questions to ask when evaluating a self-defense course, part 2 of 3:

7. **Must I train for years to learn to defend myself?**
   No. A basic course can offer enough concepts and
   skills to help you develop self-protection strategies
   that you can continue to build upon. Self-defense is
   not karate or martial arts training. It does not require
   years of study to perfect. Many people have successfully improvised and prevented an assault who have
   never taken a class. People often practice successful
   self-defense strategies without knowing it!

8. **If I use physical self-defense could I get more seriously hurt?** The question to answer first is what does
   "more seriously" mean? Rape survivors speak elo-
   quently about emotional hurts lasting long after physical hurts heal. Studies show a physical self-defense
   response does not increase the level of physical injury, and sometimes decreases the likelihood. Also,
   going along with the attacker does not guarantee that
   you will not be brutally injured anyway. The point
   of using self-defense is to de-escalate a situation and
   get away as soon as possible. Knowing some physi-

cal techniques increases the range of possible self-defense options, but the decision to choose a physical option must remain with the person in the situation.

9. **What does "realistic" mean?** Words like "most realistic," "best," "guaranteed success" etc., are all advertising gimmicks. Choosing a self-defense class is a serious decision and is preferably based on some research. No program or instructor can replicate a "real" assault, since there are so many different scenarios, and because a real attack would require a no-holds-barred fight which would be irresponsible and extremely dangerous to enact. Responsible self-defense training requires control. It is important that each student is able to control her own participation in the class and never feel forced to participate.

10. **What is the role of mace or other aggressive "devices" as self-defense aids in harming an attacker?** Any device is useless to you unless you understand how to use it, and you have it in your hand ready to use at the time of the attempted assault. There is nothing guaranteed about any of these devices. None are foolproof. None of them can be counted on to work against all possible attackers (no matter what the labeling may state to the contrary). Realize that anything you can use against an attacker can also be taken away and used against you. While some of these devices have sometimes helped women escape to safety, it is important to be aware of their limitations and liabilities.

Prepared for the National Coalition Against Sexual Assault by the NCASA Self-Defense Ad-Hoc Committee. NCASA encourages the dissemination of this material with attribution to: National Coalition Against Sexual Assault, P.O. Box 21378, Washington, D.C. 20009

Strategy #20
PUSH HANDS TECHNIQUE

Sometimes a person will grab your hand or your arm in order to make you listen to him or to gain physical control over you. You may be disagreeing with your boyfriend when he grabs you to shake you. You may be saying you don't want to fight when he grabs you to get in your face. You may be walking away from an argument when he reaches out and grabs you in order to make you stay.

This is not okay. It demands an immediate response.

If you want to be nice, you can say in a firm voice, "Let go of me," while yanking your arm from his grasp. It's not easy to hang on to someone who is yanking her arm away. This works more often than you would think, and it also works against unknown men who might grab you to get your attention. For example, in a bar it is not OK for a man to grab you as you're walking by, and it demands a response, and *not* a sultry, seductive, "What do you want, baby?" kind of response.

If that doesn't do the trick, then keep your hands open and shove against his chest (if he's that close) or push away the arm he has grabbed you with, pulling your arm free as you strike. Do it quickly and like you mean it, while shouting (or at least saying firmly), "Don't touch me like that."

Be aware that if someone intends to physically harm you, they may not back away when you do this technique. You need to stay alert to that possibility and look for the opportunity to make a safe exit. More often than not, the man will say something like, "Jeez, you don't have to get so upset, I was just trying to get your attention." In which case you respond, "It's not okay to grab me for any reason."

TIP: I've had women grab me this way, so it's not just a male action, and it's for basically the same reason: to demand my attention in an inappropriate way. Use the same technique no matter what gender the offender is. However, using a physical technique like this one sometimes escalates the tension, and your attacker may try to grab you again. That doesn't mean you shouldn't use a physical technique, only that you should be prepared. Remember: you're not to blame for the situation. The person mistreating you is.

WHY THIS WORKS: Someone who has grabbed your arm has already violated your space. He is acting in an intimidating, threatening manner. It's not an overreaction to respond immediately with a physical action of your own. Acting immediately to set boundaries and to show you're willing to defend yourself will often cause the attacker to back off. Remember to say what you want at the same time. ("Let go of me," or "leave me alone.")

• Refer to Guarded Fighting Stance, #28, and other strategies for physical techniques that you might need to use next.

Questions to ask when evaluating a self-defense course, part 3 of 3:

11. How much should I pay? Paying a lot of money for a course does not mean that you automatically get better instruction. On the other hand, don't assume that all programs are the same and go for the cheapest. It is always beneficial to be an educated consumer. Shop around as you do when buying anything that is important to you.

12. Where can I find a self-defense class? Check with your local rape crisis center. Some centers provide self-protection classes or can refer you to one. YWCAs and community colleges sometimes offer classes. Some martial arts schools provide seminars and workshops. Check the phone book. If there isn't one in your community, get involved and try to organize one.

13. Am I too old? Out of shape? What if I have some disabilities? You don't have to be an athlete to learn how to defend yourself. A good program is designed to adapt to every age and ability and provides each student with the opportunity to learn. Each individual is unique, and students should be able to discuss their own needs. Some programs have specialized classes for specific groups.

14. How can I tell a "good" course from a "bad" one? A good course covers critical thinking about defense strategies, assertiveness, powerful communication skills, and easy-to-remember physical techniques. The instructor respects and responds to your fears and concerns. Instruction is based on the belief that we can act competently, decisively, and take action for our own protection. Essentially, a good course is based on intelligence and not muscle. It offers tools for enabling a person to connect with her own strength and power. These courses are out there. Good luck in your research. Taking a self-defense class is one of the most positive things you can do for yourself!

Prepared for the National Coalition Against Sexual Assault by the NCASA Self-Defense Ad-Hoc Committee. NCASA encourages the dissemination of this material with attribution to: National Coalition Against Sexual Assault, P.O. Box 21378, Washington, D.C. 20009

Strategy #21

PROJECTING A CONFIDENT YOU

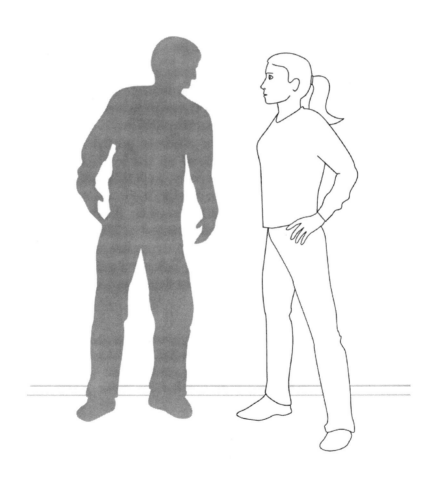

Attackers choose victims carefully. They look for people who seem distracted and vulnerable, people whom they think can be manipulated and forced to submit. If someone harasses you, do not smile or laugh nervously, even if the stranger smiles at you (perhaps trying to lull you into thinking he's friendly). See Stop Smiling, #19. Even if you're shaking on the inside, project a confident image on the outside.

- Look people in the eye as you go about your everyday business.

- Move confidently, as if you know where you're going, even if you don't.

- Keep your facial expressions calm and neutral during stressful encounters.

- Stay focused on what you're doing instead of getting distracted, but at the same time, remain aware of your environment.

TIP: Act the way you want to appear, even if you don't really feel that way inside.

WHY THIS WORKS: Attackers prefer easy victims to hard victims. If they think you'll stop them, put up a fight, draw attention to what they're doing, etc., they'll probably find someone else to pick on. Projecting self-confidence also helps you feel powerful in any self-defense situation, too.

Strategy #22

CLEARING YOUR MIND

Staying alert and mentally prepared helps you handle threats. When you're confronted by a threat, you may panic, feel fearful or become angry. None of these emotions will help you decide what to do next. Deliberately clearing your mind, however, will help you focus on doing what needs to be done.

- Stop whatever else you're doing and focus on the threat.

- Take a deep breath and push all unproductive thoughts – fear, anger and doubt – out of your mind.

- Assess the situation and decide what needs to be done. Look at the attacker while thinking of viable targets or escape opportunities. This helps keep you focused.

- Clearing your mind also requires steering clear of drugs and alcohol. You can't make good decisions if your thinking is impaired.

TIP: In everyday stressful situations, take a moment to clear your mind of fear, doubt and anger. Take a deep breath and focus on solving the problem or simply reducing your stress level. This practice will help you be mentally prepared when you face a serious threat.

WHY THIS WORKS: Effective self-defense requires the ability to act quickly on a threat. This means you have to perceive the threat and have a plan for dealing with it. By keeping your mind clear and focused, you can be effective. If you're panicked and doubtful, it's unlikely you'll be able to handle the situation as well.

Strategy #23
WALKING AWAY

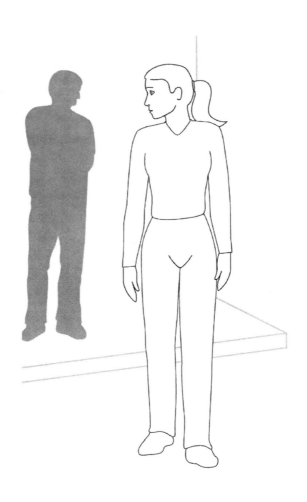

Disagreements often escalate because the people involved don't exercise self-control. If you can demonstrate self-control and simply walk away, you will not only take yourself out of harm's way, but you can also defuse the tension and stop the fight.

- Leave when you feel uncomfortable. If you get on a train and the other occupants make you feel uneasy, quickly exit the train. If you step into a parking lot and you feel nervous, walk back into the building.

- Walk away from threats and harassment if you can safely do so. If a stranger wants to talk, leave the area. If a friend is losing his temper, walk away. Discuss the matter later when everyone is calm.

TIP: If you can't walk away safely — if you feel you may be attacked, or there's no immediate safe haven — don't do it. Try to get help some other way, such as by shouting or using your cell phone, and consider what else you can do to stay safe (see Focusing on What You Can Do, #25).

WHY THIS WORKS: You can't get hurt if you're not there. Especially in cases where escalating tempers are involved, giving everyone a chance to cool off can be the very best thing to do.

Strategy #24

USING THE ENVIRONMENT

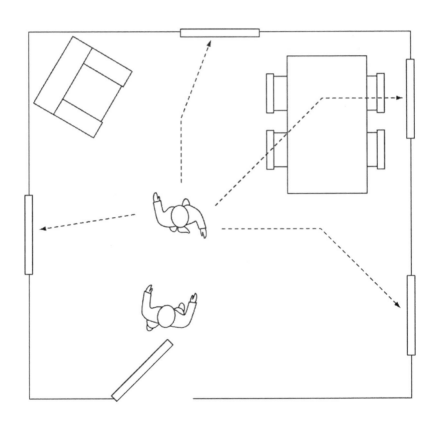

Your surroundings offer many tools for self-defense. Learn to be aware of your surroundings (see Test Your Awareness, #2) and you can use that awareness to your benefit.

- When in a new environment, determine where the exits are, identify an escape route, and locate phones and other items that could be useful if you were threatened.

- In your home and other spaces you spend a lot of time in, plan how you would escape if someone came in and identify items that you could use to defend yourself.

- If attacked, use the items in the environment. Shove the attacker against the brick wall. Pick up the fireplace poker and use it as a weapon. Throw rocks and sand at the attacker.

TIP: Be aware that an attacker can also use the environment against you. If you can use the fireplace poker as a weapon, so can he. By thinking about your environment in advance, you can also try to prevent your attacker from using the environment against you.

WHY THIS WORKS: Your environment can work for you or against you in a self-defense situation. If you don't know where the stairs are, you have no choice but to use the elevator. If you don't know where the rear exit is, you'll have to go out the front door. By understanding your environment – and also how an attacker could use it against you – you can more readily execute an effective self-defense strategy.

Strategy #25

FOCUSING ON WHAT YOU CAN DO

Often, fear makes you panic about what you can't do ("He's blocking the doorway and I can't get out"), but effective self-defense requires you to focus on what you *can* do. By focusing on your options for defending yourself, you can choose a self-defense technique that is appropriate for the situation at hand.

- Push all your emotions away (see Clearing Your Mind, #22). Focus on the situation and what you can do to escape.

- Be creative. If you're in a deserted office building and there are no co-workers to hear your calls for help, you could alert the security guard, set off a fire alarm, or escape down the back stairs.

- Be prepared to use physical techniques. If your attacker ignores your verbal boundary setting, kick him in the groin and get away.

- Do the unexpected. Play along with your attacker, pretend to faint, or pee all over your shoes. All of these techniques have worked in self-defense situations.

TIP: With a friend, ask questions like, "What if someone grabbed you in a parking garage?" Instead of just one or two ideas, think of 12 or 15 ways you could respond.

WHY THIS WORKS: If you focus on *can't*, you'll paralyze yourself and make it impossible to do any kind of action. In most self-defense situations, the ability to act, and to act quickly, is imperative. Focusing your mind on potential courses of action is more helpful than freezing and focusing on negative thoughts and outcomes.

Strategy #26

WAITING FOR YOUR OPENING

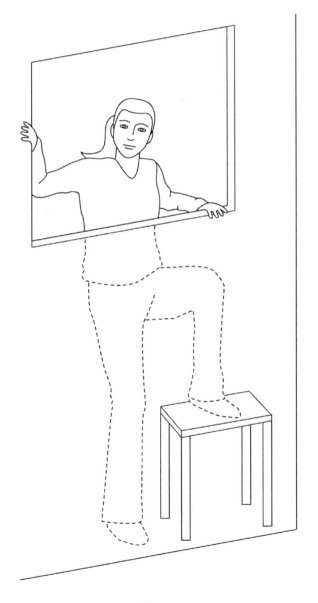

Although it's ideal to act at once when attacked or threatened (see Act Immediately, #15), sometimes an attacker takes you by surprise, and you can't or don't act immediately. You can still practice effective self-defense, however, by looking for an opening, an opportunity to use a technique to get away safely.

- Limit the chances you'll be taken by surprise by taking steps to prevent danger. Lock your doors and make visitors identify themselves before opening the door. If you must park in the parking garage, be prepared — it could be a dangerous place.

- Use the first opportunity to escape to safety. A battered woman may not dare leave her husband on an ordinary day, for example, but she might go to the shelter when he's on a business trip. If you're in a car, maybe you can jump out at the stoplight. In a house or other building, maybe you can climb out the window.

- When your attacker makes a move and gets closer, kick him, bite him, or slap him.

- Act when the attacker is distracted. Distract him yourself if you can.

TIP: Don't focus on missed opportunities. Don't waste time worrying that "If I had only done X, Y would not be happening." Wait for your next opening and take advantage of it.

WHY THIS WORKS: Like Focusing on What You Can Do, #25, Waiting for Your Opening is about keeping your mind focused on how you're going to escape the situation instead of dwelling on what you coulda, shoulda or woulda done. Being alert to every opportunity means that when an opening presents itself, you'll be ready for it.

Strategy #27

MAKING THE ATTACKER IDENTIFY WITH YOU

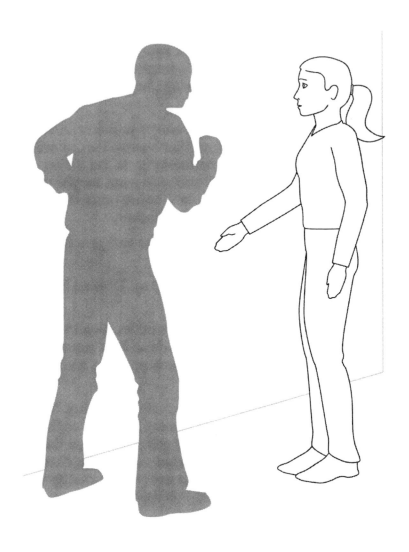

Let your assailant know that you're a person, not an object or the enemy. Only by objectifying (dehumanizing) or blaming you can most people commit violence. Making the assailant realize that you're just like him can convince him to stop the attack, or create an opportunity for you to escape.

- Look him in the eye. The attacker needs to see that you're a person like he is.

- Say, "I don't understand why you're doing this to me." If he says, "It's your fault for making me so mad," you can respond with, "I'm sorry I made you mad. I don't like it when people make me mad."

- Emphasize your similarities, saying things like "I used to have a car like this," or "This is my son's favorite song." If you can find a connection, comment on it.

TIP: Some people have successfully used appeals such as, "I have young children at home who need me. Do you have children?" or "My elderly parents depend on me. They won't know what to do without me."

WHY THIS WORKS: Many people have difficulty attacking or hurting others without blaming the other person for the violence or the problem that led to the violence. If the attacker blames you and considers you less human or less important then it's easier for him to hurt you. By making him see that you're like him, he may have more difficulty following through with his intentions. Also, by giving empathy to his situation, you make yourself seem less to blame for his predicament (though you're never to blame for someone else's violence).

Strategy #28
GUARDED FIGHTING STANCE

Take this stance when you feel physically threatened so that you are ready to protect yourself and fight back. Being on your guard communicates to yourself and to a potential attacker that you know what you're doing and you're prepared to defend yourself.

- Stand with your feet comfortably apart, your weight resting evenly between them. Place your weight forward on your toes instead of back on your heels so that you can move around more easily.

- Turn your chest slightly away from the attacker to make the target area smaller.

- Make your hands into fists and hold them up near your chin to protect your head. This puts your hands in the proper position for blocking.

TIP: Keep your body relaxed but not floppy. Be prepared to tighten up at the last minute to protect yourself from a strike or to perform a block or counterattack.

WHY THIS WORKS: Putting yourself in a position in which you can physically defend yourself prepares you for what may happen next.

Strategy #29

HIGH BLOCK AGAINST STRIKE

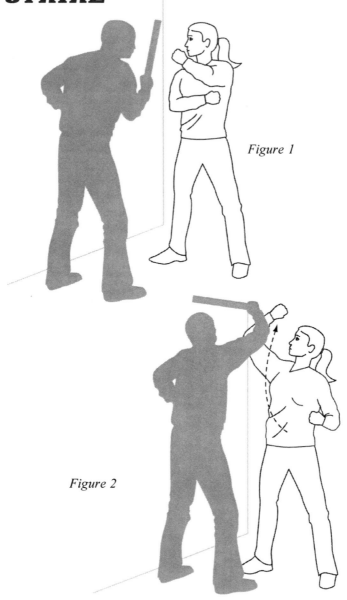

Figure 1

Figure 2

Use this technique to protect your head and face from overhead (downward) attacks. The sweep of this block deflects any strike coming down toward your head or face.

Figure 1:

- Starting in the Guarded Fighting Stance (#28) and keeping your hands in fists, bend one arm (your blocking arm) so that your forearm is parallel to the ground.

Figure 2:

- Sweep your blocking arm up in front of your body so it stops just above your head. You should be able to see out from under it.

- As you sweep your arm, twist it so that the fleshy underside of your forearm does the blocking.

TIP: Don't leave the high block in place for too long, as it exposes your rib cage, a vulnerable spot. Use it when you sense a strike coming down at your head, then bring your blocking arm back to the Guarded Fighting Stance position (see #28), with your hands resting near your chin.

WHY THIS WORKS: Your arm blocks and deflects the power of the blow, keeping your head and upper body safe from injury.

Strategy #30

LOW BLOCK AGAINST KICKS

Figure 1

Figure 2

The sweep of this block deflects a kick or other strike aimed at your lower body, including your abdomen and knees.

Figure 1:

- Starting in the Guarded Fighting Stance (#28) and keeping your hands in fists, bend one arm (your blocking arm) so that your fist touches your opposite shoulder.

Figure 2:

- Sweep your blocking arm down and across your body, unbending your elbow as you sweep.

- As you sweep your arm, twist it so that the fleshy underside of your forearm does the blocking.

- Stop the block just beyond your knee.

TIP: A quick low block has more force than a slow one and is also more likely to deflect the kick before it reaches your body, so move as quickly as you can. Keep your nonblocking hand up to protect your head and bring your blocking hand back up as quickly as possible.

WHY THIS WORKS: Rather than absorbing the strike with your body, you move all the strike's energy away from you.

Strategy #31

LEG BLOCK AGAINST STRIKES

Use this technique to protect your knees and ribs from a strike. Lifting your leg and bending your knee help you use your large, heavy thigh muscle to block an attacker's kick or a strike with a body part or even a weapon. Using your elbow to supplement the block helps you protect your body from a deflected kick.

- As the strike comes, lift your leg, bending your knee sharply. Use your outer thigh to block the strike. You may need to rotate on your supporting foot to position your body correctly.

- Keep your hands up to guard your midsection.

- From this position, you can counterattack with a Side Kick to Knee or Ribs (see #57), using your blocking leg to kick the attacker.

TIP: Practice balancing on one leg so that you can do this technique without falling over.

WHY THIS WORKS: This technique effectively protects vulnerable parts of your anatomy, such as your abdomen and lower ribs.

Strategy #32

KNIFE HAND BLOCK AGAINST STRIKES

Figure 1

Figure 2

Follow these steps to protect your midsection from a strike.

Figure 1:

- Form your blocking hand into a knife shape by flattening your hand, keeping your fingers close together. Bend your fingertips slightly.

- Move your blocking hand to the opposite shoulder, your open palm facing you. Keep your elbow bent at a 45° angle.

Figure 2:

- Sweep your arm away from your body, keeping your upper arm parallel to the floor.

- Twist your wrist at the end of the block so that your palm faces away from you.

TIP: Make sure you can see over the top of your fingers at the end of the block.

WHY THIS WORKS: As your arm sweeps away from your body, it deflects strikes aimed at your chest and ribs.

Strategy #33

ATTACKING THE VITAL POINTS

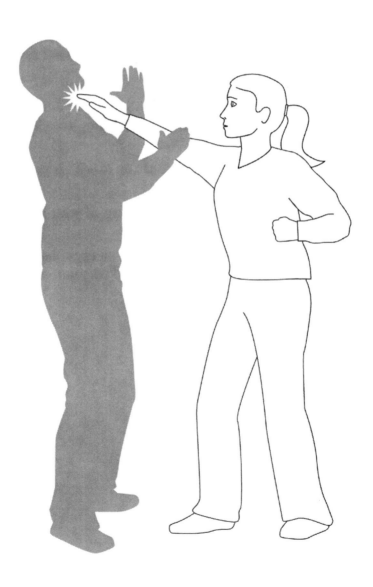

The vital points are more easily damaged than other parts of the body. This means that you can often disable, defeat, or get away from an attacker by striking these areas.

- Learn about the most vulnerable parts of an attacker's anatomy, including the eyes, throat and (for men) groin.

- Target these vulnerable areas when you must use physical techniques against an attacker. Kick the groin (see Front Kick to Groin or Ribs, #41), scratch and gouge the eyes (see Scratching and Biting, #43), or attack the throat (see Knife Hand Throat Strike, #46).

TIP: Don't focus solely on the groin. Many male attackers realize that this is a vulnerable spot and will take steps to protect it. They may even wear a protective cup, like athletes do. Consider targeting other vulnerable parts of the anatomy, such as the knees or ribs.

WHY THIS WORKS: A strong blow to the hip won't stop an attacker the same way that a hard kick to the groin or a punch to the throat will.

Strategy #34
PALM STRIKE

Use this technique to target any area on the attacker's body, including the chin, the throat, or the hand that is grabbing you. The palm strike is a simple technique that moves directly to the target area, so there's less chance of missing it. Although it's ideal to strike with the heel of your hand, striking with the palm can be effective, too.

- Flatten your hand. Keep your palm open and your fingers tightly together. Bend your fingertips slightly. The heel of your hand is the striking surface.

- Start with your hand drawn close to your body, fingertips pointing down.

- Thrust your hand to the target, twisting your wrist at the last minute so that your fingertips point up. This twist adds impact to your strike.

TIP: Turn at the hips as you strike, putting the entire weight of your body behind the blow.

WHY THIS WORKS: Because you're striking with a large surface area—the entire hand, if needed—your strike can still be effective even if not perfectly executed.

Strategy #35
PUNCH

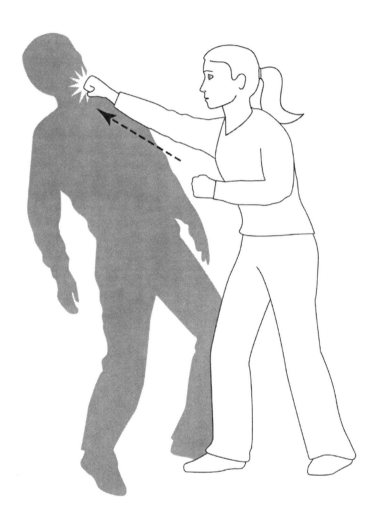

A punch uses the entire mass of your body to strike the attacker.

- Make your hand into a fist by rolling your fingers up into your hand. "Secure" them by placing your thumb across them. The knuckles of your first and middle fingers are the striking surface.

- Position your fist so that your forearm and fist are on the same flat plane, without your fist tilting up or down.

- Pull your fist back to your waist with the palm facing up.

- Thrust your fist toward the target, twisting your hand just before impact so your palm faces down.

TIP: Rotate your hips into the punch for added impact.

WHY THIS WORKS: A punch can do a lot of damage, particularly when directed toward a vital point (see Attacking the Vital Points, #33). A punch can also distract your attacker, allowing you an opportunity to escape.

Strategy #36

FOREARM BAR AGAINST GRABS

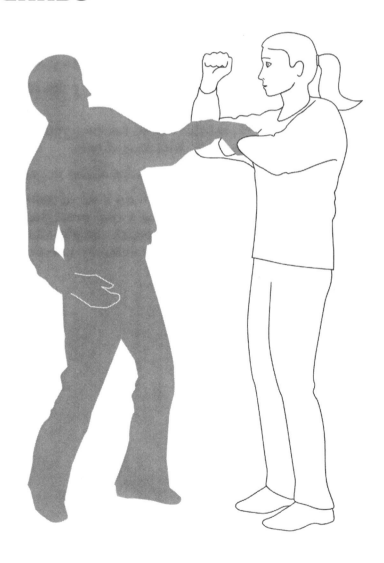

Use this method to force an attacker to release his grasp on your arm.

- Make your free hand into a fist. Keeping your upper arm parallel to the floor, bend your elbow at a 90° angle.

- Bring your arm back behind you, twisting your upper body away from the attacker.

- Sweep your arm across your body, untwisting as you go (think of a spring being released).

- Strike the attacker's grabbing arm with your forearm as forcefully as you can.

TIP: Speed is everything. A quick and powerful strike will ensure that he releases his grip. If you move too slowly, you will push the assailant's arm instead of striking it, and he may be able to resist the motion.

WHY THIS WORKS: The forearm bar dislodges the attacker's grip using momentum and mass. He cannot keep his grip if your forearm strike is forcing his arm in the opposite direction.

Strategy #37

FORWARD ELBOW STRIKE

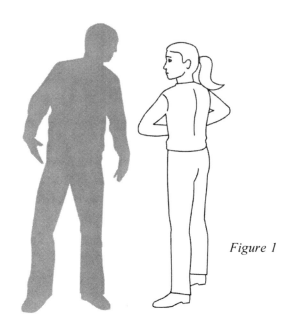

Figure 1

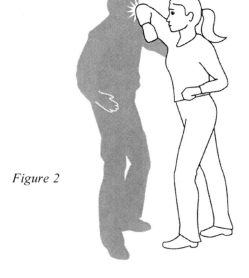

Figure 2

Use this technique to strike an assailant's head or throat.

Figure 1:

- Make your hand into a fist and bend your arm sharply, keeping your bent arm parallel to the ground. The surface just in front of your elbow is the striking area.

- Twist your upper body so that the tip of your elbow points behind you.

Figure 2:

- Unwind your torso, sweeping your arm across your body, and strike the target.

TIP: You can use a modified version of this technique even if you don't have a lot of room to maneuver. When in a small space, for example, you can swing your elbow directly into the attacker's chin without twisting your upper body back.

WHY THIS WORKS: Your elbow is a big, hard surface, so a sweeping elbow strike feels almost like getting kicked and can disorient or disable an attacker.

Strategy #38

REAR ELBOW STRIKE

If someone grabs you from behind, you need to break free in a hurry. Don't wait until he has shoved you into a waiting car or thrown you to the floor. The reverse elbow strike (so called because you're striking behind you with your elbow) is an excellent way to loosen an attacker's grip and get free.

- To do the reverse elbow strike, bend your arm tightly, making your hand into a fist. Keep your forearm parallel to the floor.

- Drive the point of your elbow into the attacker's solar plexus (between the belly button and the breast bone).

- Repeat as needed.

You can use your opposite hand to assist the elbow strike. Push the fist on your striking arm with your opposite hand. The pushing technique helps you turn your body into the strike, adding more force to it and helping you to twist free of the attacker. Once you've loosened the attacker's hold, you can pull free and get away.

TIP: It's best to practice this strike a couple of times with a friend to understand the mechanics of it and to know where to find the solar plexus. Don't go full force with the friend. Save that for the heavy bag or a padded target.

WHY THIS WORKS: A blow to the solar plexus can disorient an attacker and leave him gasping for air. This gives you a chance to get away. The point of the elbow can do a lot of damage, causing the attacker to retreat or giving you the opening you need to get away.

Strategy #39
KNEE STRIKE

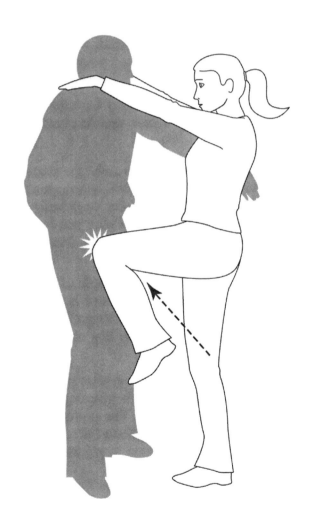

Use this technique to target the solar plexus or groin when facing an attacker.

- Stand on one leg and bend the knee of the opposite leg to a 90° angle.

- Swing your leg back, then bring it up and drive your knee into the target.

TIP: If possible, grab the attacker's shoulders, upper arms or head and pull him into the strike. If he is moving toward you and your knee is moving toward him, a head-on collision occurs, increasing the effectiveness of the blow.

WHY THIS WORKS: Your leg is heavy and powerful, and driving all that mass and energy into the attacker causes a lot of pain. And since your knee is the striking surface, all the force is concentrated into one relatively small area.

Strategy #40

STOMPING KICK

Have you ever dropped a can of peaches on your foot? Then you know that this technique, used when an attacker grabs you from behind, really hurts.

- Stand on one leg, raising the opposite leg and bending your knee.

- Thrust the heel of your foot repeatedly into the attacker's instep (the top of his foot), stomping as hard as you can.

TIP: You can also scrape the back of your heel down your attacker's shin as you stomp on his foot. His reaction will be to pull his legs away from you, throwing him off balance.

WHY THIS WORKS: Stomping on the attacker's foot, especially more than once, distracts and disorients him as he focuses on not getting stepped on. You can use the opportunity for escape.

Strategy #41

FRONT KICK TO GROIN OR RIBS

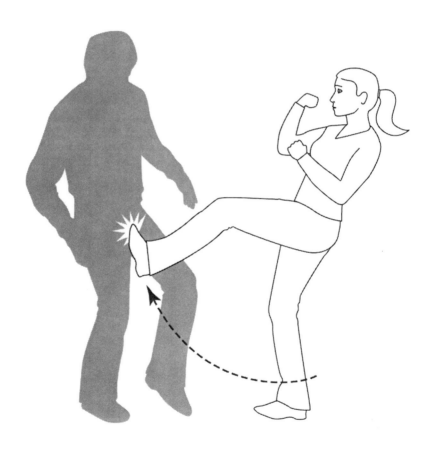

Use this kick to strike an attacker's groin when you're facing him. The groin is a vulnerable spot for men and also a sensitive area on women, so targeting it makes good sense. You can also target the ribs if the man is protecting his groin or if you think a female attacker won't be stopped by a kick to the groin.

- Stand on one leg and lift your opposite leg, bending your knee to a 90° angle. Your thigh should be parallel to the floor.

- Point your foot and pull your toes back. The ball of your foot is the striking surface.

- Thrust your foot into the target, either the groin or the ribs.

- Strike as quickly as you can, then pull your leg back before the attacker can grab it.

TIP: When wearing heavy shoes, pointing your foot and pulling your toes back is unnecessary. Strike with the entire bottom of your foot in that case.

WHY THIS WORKS: Using a kick, unlike using a punch or a knee strike, keeps you out of grabbing range, and the power of the delivery can slow or even stop your attacker.

Strategy #42

BACK FIST STRIKE TO TEMPLE

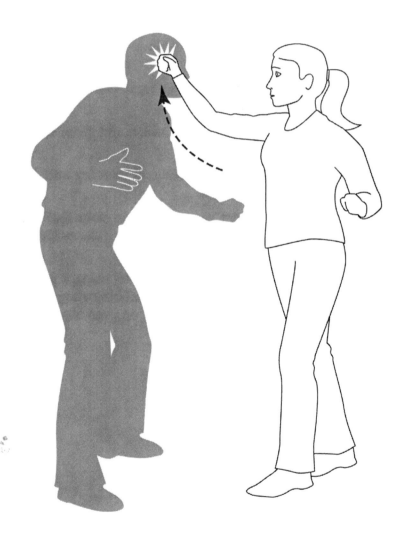

Use this technique if you're within punching range of your attacker.

- Make your hand into a fist. Roll your fingers into your palm and "secure" them by placing your thumb across them. The back of your fist is the striking surface.

- Bring your hand up toward your shoulder, palm facing down.

- Sweep the back of your hand toward the target. Twist just before impact so that your palm faces out and the back of your hand connects with the target.

TIP: Using this technique, you will strike your target with the back of your hand instead of your knuckles, so you can target bony areas of the body such as the chin or head. You would injure your hand if you punched a bony target with your knuckles.

WHY THIS WORKS: The temple is a vulnerable spot, and a solid smack to it will disorient your attacker. It can also distract him, as he will try to protect his head from further attack.

SIMPLE *SELF-DEFENSE*

Strategy #43
SCRATCHING AND BITING

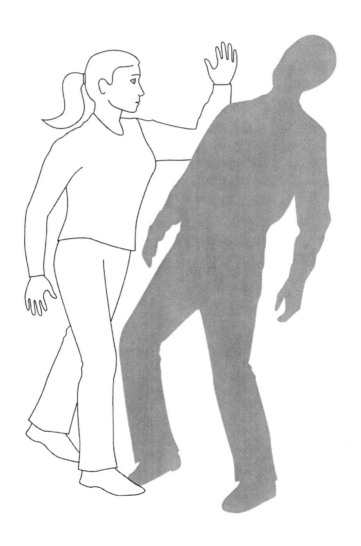

Use these techniques if you're in close or your attacker has you pinned and you can't shift him off of you.

- Claw and scratch at the attacker's face.

- Bite any part of the attacker that comes near enough, such as the fingers, arm or nose.

TIP: Keep in mind that you risk contracting a blood-borne disease if you draw your attacker's blood when biting, clawing and scratching. This risk is probably greater for biting than for scratching and clawing.

WHY THIS WORKS: An attacker may feel disoriented, vulnerable or panicked if you can draw blood. (It also demonstrates to you that your attacker is vulnerable, which may help you feel more confident about fighting.) If you bite an attacker's finger, for example, his first re-action will be to pull it away. You can use this opportunity to escape, or to further disorient and disable the attacker.

Strategy #44

APPLYING LEVERAGE AND CONSTANT MOTION

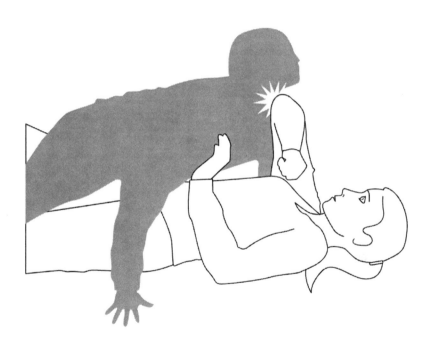

This technique is useful if your attacker has you on the ground.

- Keep moving. Move your arms, legs, head or any other part of your body that you can.

- Pinch, grab, bite, or butt heads: Do whatever you can to loosen the attacker's grip.

- Use leverage to keep the attacker off balance. Use your forearm, for example, to force his chin back, or grab his finger and pull it back.

TIP: You don't necessarily have to use a lot of physical strength. Think about dressing a squirming toddler. By the time you're through you're exhausted, but the toddler is not. Continuous motion and leverage rather than sheer force can help you in this situation.

WHY THIS WORKS: By continuously moving, squirming, and shoving the attacker, you'll constantly distract him. Keep moving and pushing (seeking leverage), and you can eventually create an opportunity to roll free, get to your feet, or otherwise escape.

Strategy #45

TIGER CLAW DEFENSE

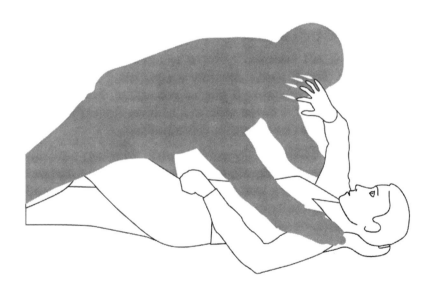

Use this defense when your body is pinned but your hands are mobile. Nails hurt when they dig into tender flesh.

- Make your hand into a claw, bending your fingertips so that your nails are exposed.

- Grab with your "tiger claws" into the attacker's soft tissue, such as their throat, eyes or cheeks.

- Use any opening created to escape.

TIP: Don't forget to shout while you're defending yourself. Roaring like a lion when you're using the tiger claw defense will surprise and distract your attacker.

WHY THIS WORKS: When you use this technique the attacker will try to move out of the way or to shift his position to trap your hands. This may create an opportunity for you to roll away and get clear.

Strategy #46

SPEAR HAND THROAT STRIKE

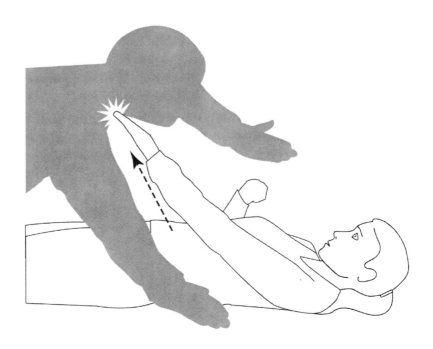

Use this technique when you are pinned but have at least one hand mobile.

- Form one hand into a spear-hand shape by flattening your hand, keeping your fingers close together. Your hand should remain rigid. Shove your fingers into the side or base of the attacker's throat.

TIP: If you can, use both hands at the same time to create an even more disorienting experience for the attacker.

WHY THIS WORKS: The throat is a vulnerable area, and any attack to it can disable the attacker. Shoving your spear hand into the attacker's throat can frighten him and cause difficulty breathing.

Strategy #47
HEAD BUTTS

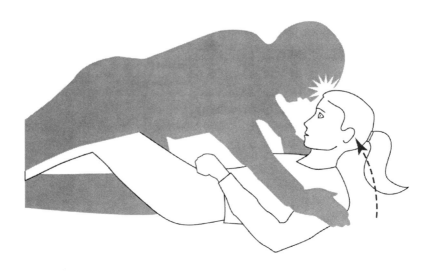

The following steps can be followed when you are pinned and have no limbs free.

- Lean your head back.

- Drive your forehead forward into the target.

- Try to strike a vulnerable spot, like the attacker's nose, rather than a hard spot, like the attacker's chin. If you hit a hard spot, the head butt could make *you* dizzy.

TIP: You can also use the back of your head to strike under the attacker's chin, possibly causing him to bite his tongue or become distracted so that you can get out of his grasp.

WHY THIS WORKS: Any strike to the head with a hard implement (in this case, your own head) can make the attacker momentarily dizzy, allowing you an opportunity to escape. Blows to the nose are particularly painful and disorienting.

Strategy #48

MULTIPLE ATTACKERS
SURVIVAL STRATEGY

To survive an attack by multiple assailants, you need to apply more than one strategy. You may be able to create an opening for escape if you keep moving.

- Try to avoid walking near groups, especially groups of young men. Don't be embarrassed to cross to the other side of the street, go back into the store, or run to your car. By avoiding the group, you may avoid an attack.

- If you feel threatened or are assaulted, try to attract as much attention as possible so that bystanders don't mistake you for part of the group or think that you're just playing around. Shout, "No," "Leave me alone" and "Back off" to establish your boundaries and to alert others.

- Stay out of the middle of the group. Keep moving so that no more than one member of the group can reach you at a time.

TIP: Group attackers aren't always encountered on the street. At a party, fraternity or nightclub, look around to make sure you know other people. If you realize that you're alone, leave.

WHY THIS WORKS: Being aware of the dangers of groups can help you avoid getting targeted by one.

Strategy #49
OUTSMARTING THE GROUP

Groups often feel invulnerable because there is power in numbers, but they forget that brains are more powerful than brawn. Outsmart them.

- Focus on ways that you might escape.

- Going alone with one member may be preferable to staying with the entire group, because it's easier to get away from one person.

- Negotiate. Ask what they want. Figure out how to give it to them or seem to give it to them without causing harm to you.

TIP: Remember that a group is only as smart as its dumbest member. Don't let the fact that there's more than one person confronting you make you freeze. You can outthink the dumbest member of the group.

WHY THIS WORKS: Groups expect you to be too frightened to act if you're by yourself or badly outnumbered. They won't expect you to fight or to plan ways to escape, or to be successful – but you can be.

Strategy #50
CREATING ALLIES

Individuals in a group often get caught up in doing something that they would never do on their own. If you can determine which member of the group is the most reluctant participant, you may be able to create an ally and use him to get away.

- Look the attackers in the eye. Force them to acknowledge that you're a person just like they are.

- Try to find the weakest link. This person may be a reluctant participant and may be able to help you. The person hanging back, looking away or seeming detached may be the weakest link.

- Ask the most reluctant member, "Why are you doing this? You don't look like the kind of person who'd be involved in something like this."

TIP: The most reluctant participant may not be the one who seems the most frightened. In fact, the most frightened person may feel that he has something to prove and must go along with the group.

WHY THIS WORKS: If you can get one person to side with you or at least refuse to go along with the group, you may be able to use the opportunity to escape.

Strategy #51

ATTACKING THE STRONGEST MEMBER

If you attack the strongest member of a group, you may alarm the weaker members. They will see that you have no fear (even if you're quaking inside), and they may be more likely to give you the opening you need to escape. If you'll fight the strongest member, the weaker ones might not want to take you on and may disperse.

- If you use a physical fight as a means to escape, try attacking the strongest member.

- Commit to the fight. Give your entire focus to disabling the strongest member.

- Realize that the other members of the group will probably move to help him. Make the fight with the strongest member quick and dirty so that the others don't have much time to react.

TIP: The strongest member of the group isn't always the biggest or most physically imposing. You need to nail the one in charge, the one whom the others seem to listen to.

WHY THIS WORKS: Showing that the ringleader is vulnerable makes all the members of the group realize they're vulnerable. They may hesitate to act or offer opportunities for escape.

Strategy #52

ATTACKING THE WEAKEST MEMBER

Attacking the weakest member of a group can help you create the opening you need to escape. It can also build your confidence. If you can look at a member of the group and tell yourself, "I can beat that little guy," you're less likely to panic. After you successfully defeat one person, then you can take on the others, if needed, or you can escape when the opportunity arises.

- If you use a physical fight as a means to escape, try attacking the weakest member.

- Commit to the fight. Focus on disabling this one attacker.

- Move quickly and fight with no holds barred. This makes it less likely the other members will jump in.

TIP: Unlike attacking the strongest member, attacking the weakest member may not cause the group to disperse, but it can still allow you the opportunity you need to escape.

WHY THIS WORKS: Showing that you're willing to fight may make the group realize you're not as easy a victim as they want. The fight itself may give you an opportunity to escape.

Strategy #53
WRIST BLOCK

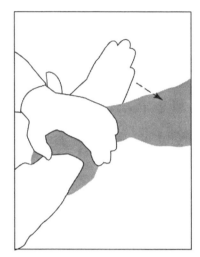

Figure 1

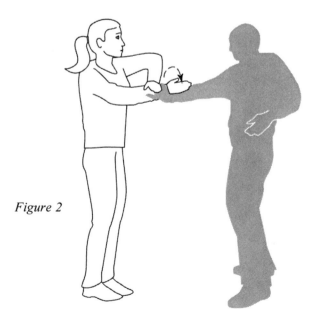

Figure 2

Use this technique when an attacker has grabbed your wrist.

Figure 1:

- Place your free hand on top of the attacker's grabbing hand.

- Form your trapped hand into a knife hand, with your palm open and fingers tight together.

- Turn your trapped hand so that your fingertips point up.

- Press the edge of your trapped hand down against the attacker's wrist.

- Force his wrist to twist by turning your trapped hand so your fingertips point down.

- Grab his wrist with your trapped hand for added leverage as you turn.

Figure 2:

- As you apply pressure, his arm will twist until his elbow faces up. You have control now. You can bring your top (free) hand back and perform a palm strike (see #34) to the attacker's elbow.

TIP: Do this technique quickly for the greatest effectiveness. This requires practice.

WHY THIS WORKS: This technique does not require a lot of strength, but uses leverage to force the attacker to release his grip or endure a lot of pain.

Strategy #54
SNAKE ARMLOCK

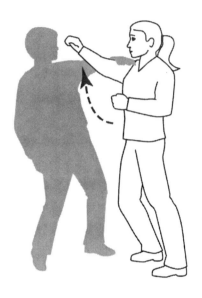

Figure 1

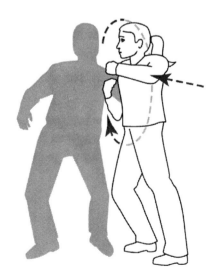

Figure 2

Use this method when an attacker has grabbed your sleeve or upper arm.

Figure 1:

- Using your arm that has been grabbed, raise your hand up and over the arm with which the attacker has grabbed you.

Figure 2:

- Scoop your raised hand under the attacker's arm, keep his arm close to you.

- Use the same arm to press up on his elbow. The higher you push his arm up, the more difficult it will be for him to maintain his balance.

TIP: Keep your free hand in a guarded position to protect yourself from his free hand. Your attacker may try to grab you to keep from falling.

WHY THIS WORKS: The snake armlock requires little weight or strength, because it uses leverage to force the attacker to release his grip on you.

Strategy #55
HAND TRAP

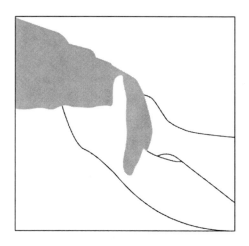

Figure 1

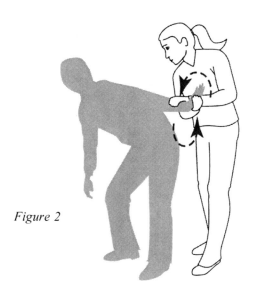

Figure 2

This is another alternative for when someone grabs your wrist.

Figure 1:

- Place your free hand on top of the attacker's grabbing hand.

- Spread the thumb of your grabbed hand away from your fingers, making a V between your thumb and index finger.

- Twist your hand so that the attacker's wrist rests in the V your hand makes. Push up on the attacker's wrist.

Figure 2:

- If the attacker doesn't let go immediately, twist your wrist down so that the V formed by your hand is inverted. The pressure of this position will force the attacker to release his grip.

TIP: Move as quickly as you can to take advantage of momentum.

WHY THIS WORKS: When an attacker has grabbed your wrist, the hand trap uses leverage to force him to release his grip. This technique requires little weight or strength.

Strategy #56

SWEEPING KICK TO KNEE

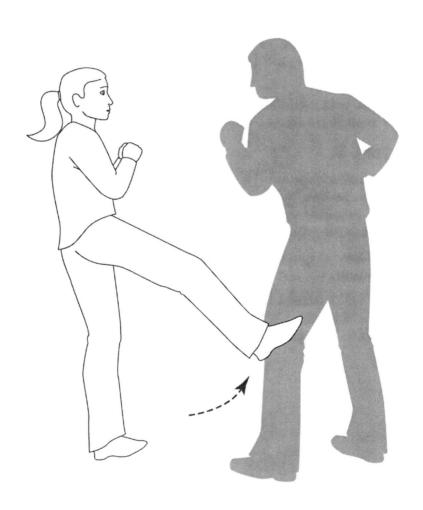

This technique is used to keep an attacker at a distance. This swift sweep is fairly simple to do, and almost anyone can manage it.

- Bend your knee to a 90° angle. Point your foot. The instep of your foot is the striking surface.

- Sweep your foot toward the attacker's knee, straightening your knee as you strike. Aim for the back of the attacker's knee.

TIP: Even if your foot doesn't land exactly where you intend it to, this kick hurts and can disorient the attacker.

WHY THIS WORKS: Your leg is the strongest and most powerful part of your body, so the force of your kick when applied to your attacker's knee should cause his knee to buckle.

Strategy #57

SIDE KICK TO KNEE OR RIBS

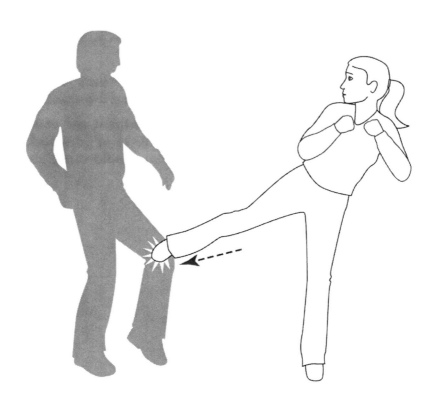

Use the side kick to keep an attacker at a distance and to break or damage the knee or ribs.

- Lift your leg that is closer to the attacker and bend the knee to a 90° angle.

- Bend your ankle so that your foot is parallel to the floor. The heel and edge of your foot are the striking surfaces.

- Turn your body so that your side faces the attacker. Your standing foot pivots as you do this.

- Thrust your kicking foot to the target, striking with your heel and the edge of your foot.

TIP: If the attacker has grabbed your hand or arm, you can use this kick by leaning away from the attacker and keeping your knee tightly bent as you lift your leg to kick.

WHY THIS WORKS: This kick has all the mass of your body behind it, so it's a powerful technique. By directing it to the attacker's knee, you can break or seriously damage his knee. Targeting his ribs can break his ribs. In either case, you'll have the opportunity to get away.

Strategy #58
ANKLE THROW

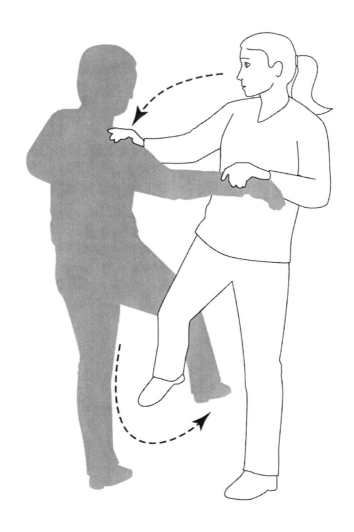

In this technique, you're using your ankle as a pivot point over which to throw an attacker. The pivot point in any throw is where you make the attacker change direction, causing him to fall or get thrown to the ground. Use this technique if the attacker is facing you and has thrown a punch or grabbed you.

- Grab one of the attacker's arms in two places: at the wrist and near the shoulder. Grabbing the clothing is fine; digging your fingernails into actual flesh is even better.

- Step forward and put your nearest foot behind the attacker's foot, your ankles touching. If stepping forward would put you in an awkward position, try sliding your nearest foot forward until it's placed behind the attacker's foot.

- Shove the attacker backward over your foot, throwing him to the ground. (No problem if he bounces.)

- Once he's on the ground, you can get away, or if you think he's going to come after you, follow up with a stomping kick, #40. He won't be so eager to go after you once you've given him a couple of broken ribs.

TIP: For this technique to work effectively, you need to do it quickly, in one lightning move, so that he doesn't catch on until he's on the ground. Otherwise, he could shove you over *his* ankle. (Not the result you were looking for.) Remember, always act decisively. An imperfect but decisive technique is 100 times better than a hesitant although technically accurate technique.

NOTE: If the attacker grabs your clothing (or has grabbed it in the first place, which is why you're doing the technique), he will often let go to try to balance himself or cushion his fall. That's the good news. The bad news is he may hang on like the grim reaper, bringing you to the ground with him. This is not ideal, but it's not the end of the world. You're on top, and you know what to expect, right? So hop to your feet before he can start grappling, and get away. Another option, if he has grabbed your clothing, is to give him a little shove to make him let go (without letting go of him) and *then* toss him over your ankle.

WHY THIS WORKS: By grabbing the attacker's arm, you make it difficult for him to react physically. Placing your foot behind his trips him up and makes him lose his balance. Since he's going backward, he'll be disoriented and trying not to get hurt. It will be difficult for him to defend against the throw.

Tips for getting the most from a martial arts or self-defense class:

Listen More Than You Talk

Sometimes the sounds of our own voices can drown out what the teacher (or a fellow student) is saying. Listen to what the teacher says. Think about it. Ask questions as needed, of course, but be sure to give all of the information you hear your full attention.

Visualize

Creative visualization can help you master the material. Picture yourself performing the techniques perfectly, then perform them. Before class, take a moment to clear your mind, and then think about having a perfect practice. After class, relax and take a moment to go over what you did and think about how you could improve your performance the next time.

Accept Criticism

If you're performing your techniques incorrectly, you need to know it. Your instructor won't be doing you any favors by overlooking poor technique just because you're a nice person. Performing techniques incorrectly can also cause damage to your body by overstressing your joints or causing strains and sprains. So when you think your instructor wouldn't know praise if it came and hit her upside the head, just remember that when you're facing a couple of street punks, you'll be glad she was hard on you.

If you really feel like your instructor only criticizes and never praises, ask him or her to tell you what you're doing right. Instructors are only human, and sometimes they forget that you need to have positive feedback, too.

Practice, Practice, Practice

Most instructors will agree that while you can get the feel for a physical self-defense technique pretty quickly, you won't actually master a technique until you have done it correctly many times. Commit to practicing physical techniques regularly so that you'll have them available if you need them.

Strategy #59
HIP THROW

Follow these steps when the attacker is behind you. Using momentum and leverage, you can throw the attacker off balance.

- Reach back with your right hand and grab whatever you can get—shoulder, upper arm, clothing or hair.

- Shove your right hip into the attacker's body.

- Pivot forward, twisting at the waist.

- Pull the attacker forward as you pivot and twist.

- Once he loses his balance, let him fall.

TIP: Practice this throw the opposite way as well—reaching back with your left hand and grabbing what you can, and so on—so that you can do it from either direction.

WHY THIS WORKS: Once you get the attacker off balance and moving forward, he won't be able to defend himself against the throw and will end up on the ground.

Strategy #60

USING WEAPONS AGAINST ATTACKERS: **STRATEGY**

Having weapons such as a gun or knife available may help you deter attackers. Practicing smart weapon ownership keeps you safe, too. If you choose to own a weapon, however, you must exercise care to keep you and your family safe.

- Although some people feel that weapon ownership can help them stay safe, remember that your own weapons can also be used against you or your family members, perhaps with fatal results. Never make a decision to purchase a weapon without careful thought and discussion among family members.

- Practice all appropriate storage and safety precautions if you choose to own and use a weapon.

- Get proper training. If you don't know how to use a gun or knife, having it handy won't be helpful.

- Remember that your environment is also full of weapons you can use — and that can be used against you. A carving knife or heavy skillet, for example, can be a deadly weapon whether you or the attacker is using it.

TIP: Keeping guns in homes with small children is extremely dangerous and, if possible, should be avoided.

WHY THIS WORKS: Weapons can be used to stop an attacker from harming you. Be aware, however, that the law limits how and when you can use weapons, and using deadly force can land you in trouble, even if you did it in self-defense. Make sure you understand your local laws about weapons ownership and use.

Strategy #61

FACING ARMED ATTACKERS: DEFENSES AGAINST A KNIFE

Figure 1

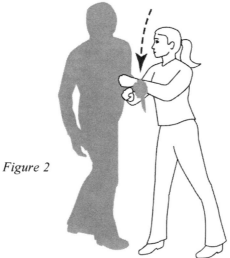

Figure 2

Defending yourself against a knife attack may require several different strategies. If you don't let the knife intimidate you, you may be able to escape safely.

- Keep the knife at a distance. Use kicks to keep the attacker from closing in.

- Protect your vital points – face, neck and abdomen – with your hands, arms, legs and feet.

- If the attacker stabs with the knife, kick his hand away.

Figure 1:

- If the attacker uses an overhead strike with the knife, block the strike by raising your arms above your head and crossing your wrists.

- Catch the attacker's *hand* (not the knife) between your wrists.

Figure 2:

- Sweep your arms across and down to position the knife away from you.

- Finish by administering a Side Kick to Knee or Ribs (see #57) or by thrusting your knee into the attacker's elbow, forcing him to drop the knife.

TIP: Fighting someone with a weapon is risky. However, not fighting them may be much riskier.

WHY THIS WORKS: An attacker with a weapon believes the weapon will intimidate you and, failing that, can be used to hurt you. By taking steps, you may be able to neutralize this advantage.

Strategy #62

FACING ARMED ATTACKERS: DEFENSES AGAINST A STICK OR BAT

Defending yourself against an attack with a stick or bat may require several different strategies. Not being intimidated by the weapon can help you escape.

- Keep the weapon at a distance. Use kicks to keep the attacker from closing in.

- Protect your vital points – face, neck and abdomen – with your hands, arms, legs and feet.

- Use a forearm bar to block a strike with a stick (see Forearm Bar Against Grabs, #36).

- Bend your elbow at a 90° angle, then sweep your arm toward the stick. Twist your arm so the fleshy side of your forearm blocks the strike.

- Use the hand of your blocking arm to grab the stick.

- Follow up with punches and kicks to disable the attacker.

- Use a High Block Against Strikes (see #29) if the attacker is swinging downward with the stick, aiming for your head.

TIP: Blocking with the fleshy part of your arm minimizes the likelihood of damage to you.

WHY THIS WORKS: As with a knife or gun, an attacker with a weapon believes the weapon will intimidate you and, failing that, can be used to hurt you. By taking steps, you may be able to neutralize this advantage.

Strategy #63

FACING ARMED ATTACKERS: DEFENSES AGAINST ENVIRONMENTAL WEAPONS

Environmental weapons fall into three categories: throwing, stabbing and striking weapons. Knowing which kind of weapon your attacker is wielding will help you choose the best strategies.

- Keep the attacker at a distance. Use kicks to keep the attacker from closing in (see Front Kick to Groin or Ribs, #41 and Side Kick to Knee or Ribs, #57).

- Determine the weapon type: throwing, stabbing or striking.

- Throwing weapons (a rock, a plate) are difficult to target accurately. Get out of range quickly. Move behind an obstacle. Don't run in a straight path.

- If the object is a stabbing weapon (letter opener, scissors), use Defenses Against a Knife (see #61).

- If the object is a striking weapon (golf club, fireplace poker), use Defenses Against a Stick or Bat (see #62).

TIP: Focus on getting away from the attacker safely. If that's not possible, focus on disarming the attacker first. Then, if you must, focus on disabling him.

WHY THIS WORKS: An attacker with a weapon believes the weapon will intimidate you and, failing that, can be used to hurt you. By taking steps, you may be able to neutralize this advantage.

Strategy #64

FACING ARMED ATTACKERS: DEFENSES AGAINST A GUN

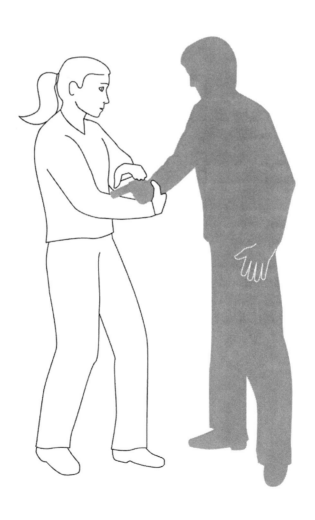

If you don't let a gun intimidate you, you may be able to escape an armed attacker.

- Most guns – and most attackers – are inaccurate against a moving target at a distance, so get away quickly. Use obstacles (a wall, a dumpster) to protect you as you move. Bend down to create a smaller target and to protect your head.

- If you are at close range, you may be able to disarm the attacker. This is an extremely dangerous maneuver to attempt. Place your right hand on top of the gun and the gun hammer (for a revolver) or the chamber (for an automatic). If the hammer or chamber is blocked, the gun cannot be fired.

- Secure the gun underneath with your left hand. If possible, place your finger behind the trigger so the trigger cannot be pulled. Twist the weapon away from your body.

TIP: Any defense against a gun is seriously risky. However, not defending yourself against a gun can be riskier.

WHY THIS WORKS: An attacker with a weapon believes the weapon will intimidate you and, failing that, can be used to hurt you. By taking steps, you may be able to neutralize this advantage.

Conclusion: From Fearful to Fabulous

In my workshops and seminars, I hear over and over again from women who want action steps to help them become stronger and more courageous. They feel that fear holds them back from living the lives they want. They talk about turning down jobs and deciding not to relocate to other cities and choosing to stay home instead of going out with friends because they're afraid of compromising their safety. They think that such actions might be too risky, and they'd be better off staying where it's safe. But they don't want to live like this anymore.

Most of us don't. We're tired of all the people who tell us we should be afraid and who think that terrorizing us with grisly crime details is an effective method of keeping us safe. We're tired of people telling us to stay inside, as if *we* were the criminals. We want to get out there and live.

But we also want to be sensible. We have lives to get on with, but we don't want to expose ourselves to unnecessary risks.

I was thinking about this the other night when I had to bring my little girl to the emergency room at the local hospital. It was late and dark and deserted, and I couldn't get a parking spot near the doors. I thought how frightened I would have been 10 or 12 years ago, before I learned the strategies for staying safe. And I realized what a gift it was that I could take my daughter to the hospital late at night and not have my worry for her health be compounded with fear over our safety. I know that there are other women who are walking across hospital parking lots right now, and they're afraid and not sure what to do. I want them to know what to do. I want them to be able to do what needs to be done, do what they want to do, and not be afraid that the consequences will be terrible.

When I was younger, I rarely did anything I really wanted to do, because I was afraid of what might happen to me. I never traveled by myself, never moved to New York, never met friends on the spur of the moment, because I was convinced I'd end up left for dead on the side of the road. I lived like that for way too long, thinking I could be safe and secure if I just never actually set foot outside my front door.

But the problem was I hated never doing what I wanted to do. I had dreams about standing up for myself and traveling to Greece with just my passport and a couple hundred bucks. But to get there, I had to learn to trust myself. I had to believe I could take care of me.

So one day, I found myself walking into a martial arts school and signing up for lessons, because I wanted, more than anything, to get out into the big bad world and see what it had to offer. I didn't want to be afraid anymore. What I learned was that I could take care of myself. I found my own power, and I started to live the life I wanted – and still stayed safe.

That's why, when I became a personal safety coach, I promised myself that I would never turn into one of those "experts" whose idea of taking care of yourself is never leaving your house except in the company of three strong men. That I wouldn't spend all my time giving asinine tips like, "Don't go out after dark." (I wonder what women in Alaska are supposed to do in the winter when it's dark 24 hours a day.) Or, "Don't go shopping by yourself." (I'm supposed to hire an escort if I want to pick up groceries on the way home from work?) I made this promise to myself and to all the women I would teach, and sometimes it has been tough going, because we're conditioned to think that to stay safe we have to stay inside. In many ways, it's what women want me to say. They want to be reassured that if they just keep their doors locked and their cell phones with them at all times, they'll be safe.

But they won't be. The only way they'll be safe is if they depend on themselves. Take care of themselves. I show them how they can learn to rely on their own brains and wits to do what needs to be done – to take care of themselves no matter what the circumstances. Whether they're lost in old city Istanbul (as I found myself one summer) or being threatened by the boyfriend they just broke up with.

When I lead personal safety and empowerment workshops, the students always ask me, "What would you do if . . ." and then they come up with some unlikely scenario (along the lines of, "You wake up tied to a tree?")

And I'll say, "Come on, no one wakes up tied to a tree, except in Hollywood movies."

And they'll insist, "Yeah, but what if?"

So I tell them that I would look for what I could do instead of what I couldn't do. And to demonstrate, I have the students – I call them Defenders – stand up and form a circle, holding hands. I put one Defender in the middle of the circle. I tell her, "Suppose you can't climb over the people's arms. Suppose you can't crawl under. Suppose you can't push your way through their arms. In fact, suppose you can't touch them at all. What do you do to get out of the middle of the circle?"

And after some minutes of head scratching, the woman in the center says what she wants: "Let me out!" And they let her out.

Of course, saying "Let me out!" may not work if someone has shoved you in the trunk of his car, but it's something you could try. It's more helpful to think of all the things you *can* do instead of all the things you *can't.*

In my training, I try to show the Defenders how to take care of themselves without having to rely on firearms, spouses, guard dogs and burglar alarms. In other words, I try to show them that what they have inside is enough. They've got the brains and creativity and guts to do what needs to be done.

They want to know how they can get out of a threatening situation without getting hurt, how they can find opportunities for safety. And let's be clear: they want strategies that have nothing to do with the usual "Look under your car before getting in," and "Have a man answer the telephone" that we've been hearing for years and which don't appear to make us any safer.

The Defenders in my workshops think maybe I know how to take care of myself in this way. And they're right. I've been training as a martial artist for nearly 15 years. But we all know how to take care of ourselves. We just don't realize it. We all have the capacity, the ability inside of us. I believe that with all my strength.

I want you to find that capacity inside you. The simple strategies in this book can help you stay out of trouble, get out of trouble and keep yourself safe from danger. They can help you learn how to spot the red flags that signal a potentially dangerous person and to understand what the real risks are. Best of all, you'll learn to trust yourself.

Women have used these strategies for years to get out of trouble – they just didn't necessarily have a name for them. I've seen these strategies in action. I've used them myself. I've backed down more than one aggressive man just by standing my ground and being prepared to do what needed to be done.

My students have told me their success stories. One reported how she was working late one evening by herself when a stranger came in and demanded that she come with him. "I just put my hands up in a guarded position, getting ready to shove him," she says, "And I shouted NO! And he left the building." This is a woman who is not even five feet tall and weighs about 90 pounds.

I also learn about others who may not have trained in self-defense but who used their brains and wits to escape a threatening situation. A recent newspaper report in my hometown described how a woman fended off a masked attacker by shouting at him to go away and moving toward a nearby road with cars traveling down it. Another woman defended herself against an attacker who grabbed her and started hitting her by shoving him away and shouting, "No!" None of these successful efforts required great brute strength or years of training. They just required a little self-confidence and the know-how we all have.

What my Defenders find most transforming about learning to take care of themselves is that it's fun being powerful. When I finally learned to stand up and defend myself, instead of locking myself indoors after dark and huddling under the covers, I stopped being afraid for the first time in my life. I stopped worrying about psycho muggers jumping out at me from the bushes (you should see what I have planned for *them*). I started having a lot of fun in life. Traveling alone, raising a child as a single mother, becoming a book author. Things I would have been afraid to do if I hadn't learned to stop being afraid.

By learning the simple strategies in this book, you can get on with the most important thing – living your most joyful, fearless life possible.

Enjoy this book?

Here are some others you might like by the same author.

Kickboxing for Women
Jennifer Lawler and Debz Buller

ISBN-13: 9781930546530 • $16.95 • 224 pages • photos • trade paper

Kickboxing for Women contains information helpful to beginning, intermediate and advanced kickboxers. It covers the principles, techniques and drills for the fitness kickboxer as well as the competitive one.

"*Kickboxing for Women* is a winning supplement to any female kickboxer's physical fitness regimen." — *Midwest Book Review*

PUNCH! Why Women Participate in Violent Sports
Jennifer Lawler, Ph.D.

ISBN-13: 9781930546509 • $16.95 • 224 pages • trade paper

"Lawler uses language that is easy to read and suitable for teenagers..." — *Today's Librarian*

"...an amalgam of personal experiences and scholarly research... An optional purchase for high school, college and public libraries." — *Library Journal*

"A thoughtful survey . . . Powerful." — *Oxygen* magazine, four stars

Tae Kwon Do for Women
Jennifer Lawler

ISBN-13: 9781930546448 • $16.95• 256 pages • 350 photos • trade paper

"Finally! What took so long? Jennifer Lawler, the author of *The Martial Arts Encyclopedia* has written a book called *Tae Kwon Do for Women* that was long overdue..."
— *Taekwondo*

"Whether you're an experienced practitioner or a newbie, Jennifer Lawler's *Tae Kwon Do for Women* will have something just for you." — *Black Belt*

Training Women in the Martial Arts
Jennifer Lawler and Laura Kamienski

ISBN-13: 9781930546844 • $16.95 • 128 pages • trade paper

Training Women in the Martial Arts is for male and female martial arts instructors, female martial arts students and supporters of women in the martial arts. The book is designed to help people involved in the martial arts understand the challenges women face when training and help them create and provide appropriate martial arts and self-defense instruction.

LaVergne, TN USA
22 February 2010
173818LV00002B/2/P